. . . And everybody can and *should* become a **CULTURE ADVOCATE.**

...lture is a system. Systems either ...power or entitle people.

DO WHAT YOU CAN WHERE YOU ARE NOW

A Culture Advocate *aligns* more and more of his or her actions with the organization's mission, priorities, and plan every day.

Committed.

COACHable.

Aware.

The *beautiful* thing about establishing a culture of coaching is that you are unleashing the incredible

POWER of the human spirit in *unimaginable ways.*

CREATE

COMMUNICATE

EXECUTE

CULTURE is the SOUL of an organization.

the culture
solution

A Practical Guide to
Building a Dynamic Culture

the
culture
solution

So People Love Coming to
Work and Accomplishing
Great Things Together!

Matthew Kelly

BLUE SPARROW
North Palm Beach, Florida

Design by Ashley Wirfel

ISBN: 978-1-63582-024-9 (hardcover)
ISBN: 978-1-63582-027-0 (e-book)
ISBN: 978-1-63582-095-9 (audiobook)

10   9   8   7   6   5   4   3   2   1

Printed in the United States of America

FIRST EDITION

table of
contents

1

everybody wants a dynamic culture

Everything Begins with a Story

In 1163 a man was walking along the river Seine in Paris when he noticed a huge new building site. He approached the site and found men laying bricks. It was late in the afternoon, and the workers were tired and sweating.

He asked one worker, "What are you building here?" He replied, "I'm just laying bricks."

He asked another worker, "What are you building here?" The worker scoffed and said to the man, "Are you blind? I'm building a wall."

Frustrated, the man began to walk away, but as he turned he bumped into one of the other men, who was also laying bricks. "What are you building here?" he asked.

The builder stopped working. He stepped back and beckoned

the man to do the same. Then, looking up toward the sky, he said, "We are building a cathedral."

"Cathedrals are beautiful," the onlooker commented.

"You have never seen a cathedral this beautiful," the bricklayer replied. "This will be the finest cathedral the world has ever seen. It will tower above the city, men and women will marvel at it, and people will come from all over the world just to see it."

It took 182 years to finish that cathedral. Those who began building it never got to see it completed. It is 420 feet long, 157 feet wide, and 300 feet high, and with all of France's rich history, incredible sights, and phenomenal art, it is still the most visited attraction in France each year. With thirteen million annual visitors, that is almost twice as many as the Eiffel Tower and four million more than the Louvre.

It is the Notre-Dame Cathedral. Men and women of all faiths and no faith come to visit Notre-Dame de Paris and marvel at it.

Do you love coming to work? Do you feel like you are accomplishing great things with the people you work with? Does your culture provide the context to make these things possible?

Your organization's culture should be something to marvel at. People should want to visit just to observe it. When they hear that you work there, they should have questions about how you created the culture so that they can emulate it themselves. The thing is—and it's quite simple, really—everybody wants to belong to a Dynamic Culture. That's why today, more than ever before, organizations are searching for a Culture Solution.

While everyone wants to belong to a Dynamic Culture, what most people don't realize is that everyone is responsible for creating one. You have a role to play. We all have a role to play. A Dynamic Culture is built one brick at a time, just like a cathedral. It doesn't just magically appear. So there is no time to waste— let's begin today and make your organization's culture not only something to marvel at, but a place where people love coming to work to accomplish great things together.

Now, these may be inspiring words for some people, but not everyone is moved by the same things. You might be reading this thinking to yourself that all this culture stuff is on the softer edge of business ideas and not really that important. Some people lean in that direction when it comes to culture, and that's OK. It's an easy mistake to make, but it *is* a mistake. If you are that person, let me demonstrate how much culture matters in another language.

Harvard conducted a study of more than two hundred organizations and discovered that a strong culture increased profits by 756 percent over a period of eleven years. Culture matters. How much? Hard to say, but I suspect if you put together a list of things that could increase your profits by more than 750 percent over the next decade, it would be a very short list.

The FLOYD Philosophy

At FLOYD Consulting, we are passionate about growing people and growing organizations. We believe the two are inseparably linked. If you don't grow your people, you cannot create long-term sustainable growth and success for your organization. At the same time, you cannot focus solely on growing your people while ignoring what has to be done today to keep the organization running.

Partnering with organizations like yours to bring out the best in everyone and everything in order to maximize people, processes, and profits (or impact in the case of a nonprofit) is our mission and passion. When you walk into our offices, there is a brushed-metal sign that reads: WE GROW PEOPLE. Helping people grow is an amazing thing. If you have children, a younger brother or sister, or nieces and nephews, you know this firsthand. Helping people grow and develop their potential is tremendously satisfying.

When you were a child, your parents didn't want you hanging out with certain kids. They told you those children were a bad influence on you. There were probably also some things your parents didn't want you doing. You probably complained and asked why, and your question was most likely met with a vague answer that didn't really satisfy you.

Parents have dreams for their children, one in particular. And they have special instincts that alert them when that dream is in danger. What's the dream? Your parents want you to become the-best-version-of-yourself. They may not have been able to articulate it in those words, but that's why they didn't want you hanging out with those kids, and why they didn't want you doing certain things or putting yourself in particular situations. They knew that those people, places, things, and situations all posed a threat to their dream for you to become the-best-version-of-yourself. This is the universal parental dream. It isn't just your parents' dream for you; it is every parent's dream. If you have children yourself, you may not have used these particular words, but in your heart, you want your children to explore their potential and become a-better-version-of-themselves each day.

Our philosophy at FLOYD Consulting is: *Your organization can only become the-best-version-of-itself to the extent that the people who are driving your organization are becoming better-versions-of-themselves.*

Since I first coined the phrase *the-best-version-of-yourself* twenty-five years ago, I have been amazed by its universality. It applies to everything, everywhere, all the time. There is no aspect of life, an organization, or society that this concept doesn't touch and animate.

Healthy food helps you become *the-best-version-of-yourself.*

A good friend helps you become *the-best-version-of-yourself.*

Reading great books helps you become *the-best-version-of-yourself.*

Travel helps you become *the-best-version-of-yourself.*

A good leader helps you become *the-best-version-of-yourself.*

Exercise helps you become *the-best-version-of-yourself.*

Hard work helps you become *the-best-version-of-yourself.*

Being patient with your child, spouse, client, or colleague helps you become *the-best-version-of-yourself.*

Everything we do every day helps us become either a-better-version-of-ourselves or a-lesser-version-of-ourselves. Some people may say it is impossible to be the-best-version-of-yourself all the time. I agree. But you can probably look back on your day yesterday and identify a moment when you were at your best. In that moment, you were the-best-version-of-yourself.

Every person in your organization is capable of being the-best-version-of-themselves for at least one moment today. That moment is like a single brick in that great cathedral in Paris. And if we can do it for one moment today, we can do it for two moments tomorrow, and ten moments next Thursday. This is how great champions are made, and how great cultures are built.

Dynamic Cultures help people to recognize the moments in a day when they were the-best-version-of-themselves, and teach them to multiply those moments in the days, weeks, months, and years ahead.

Dynamic Cultures increase cooperation, collaboration, trust, and motivation, and they are built one moment at a time. Culture builders do something every day to become a-better-version-of-themselves, and they do something every day to help the organization's culture become a-better-version-of-itself.

Everyone can do that. Nobody can say, "That's too hard," "That's too intellectual," "That's overwhelming," or "That's not my job." We are all in this together; culture building is everyone's responsibility. Every single person can be a culture builder for at least one moment each day—and that's how you transform a culture.

Will some people resist the idea? Yes. Will there be people who sabotage the effort to build a Dynamic Culture out of fear, comfort, or laziness? Absolutely. Would you let those people train the rising stars in your organization? I didn't think so. If someone were poisoning your child's drinking water, how long would you tolerate that? If you found out today that you had cancer, how long would you delay before you sought the appropriate treatment? You cannot allow disruptive personalities to kidnap your organization's culture. Cut out the cancer. Culture builders in positions of leadership act decisively with courage to protect the mission and give the organization its best chance of becoming the-best-version-of-itself.

Every organization, community, and nation organizes around a principle. The universality of this concept of striving to become the-best-version-of-ourselves transforms people, marriages, families, and communities—and it holds the power to transform your organization's culture. It will do this in a thousand ways, but let's briefly discuss three.

1. **Decisiveness.** This single principle alone makes organizations dynamic. Will what we are considering help this organization accomplish its mission and become the-best-version-of-itself? This question provides arresting clarity. Unhealthy cultures are indecisive; Dynamic Cultures are decisive.

2. **Conflict and Unity.** The-best-version-of-yourself principle creates unity by providing a common, unchanging purpose and a context for healthy conflict. Now we can argue *for something* rather than arguing *against each other.* This is no small thing. How organizations deal with conflict is one of the telltale signs of the health of their culture. If your mission is your constitution, this principle is your declaration of independence.

3. **Clarity.** The-best-version-of-yourself principle provides enduring clarity that Mission Is King. Most employees have an astounding lack of clarity about their organization's mission and what their specific role is in fulfilling that mission.

"Your organization can only become the-best-version-of-itself to the extent that the people who are driving your organization are becoming better-versions-of-themselves."

We base all our consulting, training, and coaching on this principle, the FLOYD Philosophy. And we offer it to you now as a principle to organize your Dynamic Culture around. Whatever your mission is, whatever your organization is trying to accomplish—grow your people! It is the essence of building, growing, and sustaining a dynamic organizational culture.

Culture Eats Strategy for Breakfast, Lunch, and Dinner

"Culture eats strategy for breakfast." This quote has been attributed to the great management consultant Peter Drucker, though nobody has been able to provide a citation. It certainly sounds like him. He had a dozen similar maxims:

- *"Management is doing things right; leadership is doing the right things."*
- *"The most important thing in communication is to hear what isn't being said."*
- *"There is nothing so useless as doing efficiently that which should not be done at all."*
- *"Meetings are by definition a concession to a deficient organization. For one either meets or one works. One cannot do both at the same time."*
- *"So much of what we call management consists of making it difficult for people to work."*
- *"What gets measured gets improved."*

Did he say it? Nobody knows. It doesn't matter who said it—culture is more important than strategy. You may have an amazing product and plan, but nothing will limit your organization's success like an unhealthy or dysfunctional culture. And if what you sell is a service, I suggest you become so obsessed with culture that people start to wonder if you have fallen in love or had a religious experience.

Culture does eat strategy for breakfast. It's not just a cute turn of phrase; it is absolutely true. You simply cannot create scalable and sustainable success without a Dynamic Culture.

Occasionally an organization with a massively dysfunctional culture will *appear* to be defying this truth, but the unspoken reality is: They are giving up a huge amount of upside as a result of their dysfunctional culture; their employees are paying a miserable price for the organization's success; and the organization's leadership is at best mortgaging its future and at worst raping it. In the process, they rob their employees of the joy of meaningful work and the opportunity for the reward and recognition they so richly deserve. These organizations may *seem* successful, but with a Dynamic Culture their success would be staggeringly greater.

For too many leaders, culture isn't important until it's urgent, and by the time it's urgent, it's too late. A bad culture can hide behind a great product or innovation for a while, but not forever. Unhealthy cultures can limp along, even grow moderately in an expanding industry, but before too long the employees will become miserable and disengage, and anyone with real talent will leave. The best people leave first, just like the best swimmers leave a sinking boat first. Sick cultures lose their ability to attract top talent, which means sooner or later they get stuck with second-rate, mediocre employees who go there to hide their mediocrity or laziness.

It is common for culture to be neglected in favor of strategy, especially in the short term. In small and new organizations, this is understandable. Anyone who has ever started an organization can tell you epic stories about how hard they worked to get it up and running. But while this may be necessary in the short term, it is not sustainable in the long run.

Culture is also often neglected in favor of short-term gain. The real disease sets in when culture is ignored, set aside, or neglected just for the sake of profit, bonuses, or share price. In the long run every organization pays the price for this type of shortsighted-ness. Culture is your organization's best lifelong friend.

The best thing about Dynamic Cultures is they are fertile. They procreate, and the children of great cultures are: employee engagement, trust, innovation, creativity, customer and employee loyalty, extraordinary teamwork, fun, entrepreneurialism, adaptability, and so much more. Culture—not strategy, technology, finance, industry knowledge, or marketing—is the ultimate competitive advantage of our age. It will be the organizations with the best cultures that will dominate their competition in the twenty-first century.

So, who's keeping an eye on culture in your organization? Who is responsible for intentionally developing a Dynamic Culture in your organization? When was the last time you had a proactive conversation about culture (not to be confused with a reactive conversation about culture that popped up because something went wrong or someone complained)? Does culture have a line in your budget?

The sad, tragic, miserable truth is that most organizations are very passive about culture—but Dynamic Cultures don't just happen; they are created *intentionally*. A Dynamic Culture is essential to the long-term success of any organization—isn't it time you started getting more intentional about yours?

The Promise of This Book

Every book makes a promise. Great books keep that promise. By the end of this book, I hope to have convinced you that culture should be a priority for you and your organization, whether your organization is a small business, a Fortune 500 company, a nonprofit, a school, a church or faith community, an industry association, a professional sports team, or a club of any type. It is my intention to demonstrate exactly how to go about building a Dynamic Culture that surprises and delights your employees and customers.

Whatever role you have in your organization, I will teach you how to become a Culture Advocate. In fact, just by intentionally focusing on helping your organization become a-better-version-of-itself and doing one thing each day to improve the culture, you are already so far along the path.

This book should not overwhelm you. Wherever you and your organization are in your cultural journey, this book is about taking the next small step toward establishing a Dynamic Culture. Section after section, chapter after chapter, one principle at a time, you should find yourself nodding your head and saying to yourself, "I can do that," or "We could do that in our organization." *If at any point you feel overwhelmed, you have either misunderstood the message or you are trying to force a timeline that is unreasonable.* It takes time to build a Dynamic Culture.

These are the promises I hope to live up to in writing this book for you. It is also my hope to make page after page interesting, educational, and inspiring, so that the ideas on these pages will reach deep into your life, both personally and professionally—because the ideas that impact us both personally and professionally change our lives forever.

The Most Frightening Idea in Business Today

Whatever your mission, you will need to train your people to fulfill it. There is perhaps no area of corporate life that will need to be more radically transformed over the next twenty years if organizations are going to succeed.

It is also in the arena of training that organizations have an enormous opportunity to impact the positive-to-negative ratio (which we will speak about in the next section) in ways that are literally life-changing for employees and transformational for an organization. This is not aspirational rhetoric. I have seen this with my own eyes a thousand times as organizations applied the principles from my book *The Dream Manager* in their organizations.

Five hundred years ago, businesses only thought about training people to do their work. The idea of teaching them something that might improve them as people or better their lives would have been met with blank stares.

In 1943 psychologist Abraham Maslow published his paper "A Theory of Human Motivation," which presented his theory of human development. Maslow believed that people have common needs arranged in a hierarchy, and as each of these needs is met, people grow and develop. He presented this hierarchy of needs in the form of a pyramid with five categories. From bottom to top, they are:

- **Physiological.** These needs are required simply to survive: air, water, food, shelter, and clothing.
- **Safety.** These needs include but are not limited to: physical safety, economic safety (primarily employment security), and protection from criminals and tyrants.
- **Love and Belonging.** Once a person's needs for basic survival and safety have been reasonably satisfied, convinced that our survival is not being immediately threatened, we turn outward. Here we discover the need

for friendship, community, intimacy, and family, and the need to love and be loved. And of great importance, we discover our need for acceptance and belonging.

- **Esteem.** In this fourth category is the need for respect. This includes both the respect of other people and self-respect. The latter is often more difficult to attain than the former, and the respect of every other person on the planet would not necessarily establish self-esteem or self-respect. In fact, Maslow himself referred to the esteem of others as "lower" and self-esteem as "higher." People will go to extraordinary lengths to attain fame, recognition, status, and attention. These efforts are often driven by a need for or a lack of self-respect.

- **Self-actualization.** Maslow believed that the pinnacle of humanity's needs, his fifth category, is for a person to reach his or her full potential. Perhaps his most famous quote is: "What a man can be, he must be." He estimated that only 1 percent of humanity reaches self-actualization.

The reason I mention Maslow and his hierarchy of needs is because it both changed and entrenched certain ideas about "the worker" in the minds of business owners, leaders, whole industries, and organizational life in general. Some of these changes in attitude and belief were for the better and some were for the worse.

Maslow's theory sought to explain what motivates people, but that is not our primary interest here. What is essential to understand is that somewhere around this time, due at least in part to Maslow's work, organizations began to realize that helping workers to develop as human beings—beyond what directly made them better at playing their specific roles—was good for business. Perhaps nobody would have articulated it this clearly, but the idea began to exist at least in some vague sense. Nonetheless, even in the vaguest sense it represented an enormous shift in the relationship between an organization and its workers.

Over the past seventy-five years, we have seen both the progression and regression of this idea. But if modern businesses are to thrive and if advanced nations are to increase their standard of living, it is essential that organizations take this idea very seriously again—in fact, more seriously than ever before, for these two unspoken, uncomfortable reasons: (1) the education system is failing to prepare our young people for life and work; and (2) everything everyone who works for your organization does helps it become either the-best-version-of-itself or a-lesser-version-of-itself.

1. In terms of education, I am not speaking of some bankrupt, broken-down public school system in the one of America's inner cities. I mean the education system from preschool to grad school, across the country, up and down every level, regardless of socioeconomic opportunity, advantage, or disadvantage.

America is losing its place in the world's economy because we are not sufficiently preparing or engaging our young people during the first twenty-two years of their lives. The website Ranking America places the United States at number 14 in education, 24 in literacy, 11 in fourth-grade math, 23 in the PISA science score (this one really, really matters as we look to the future), 15 for tertiary graduation rates, 18 in reading, 2 in ignorance (not sure how they measure that), 26 for employment growth rates, and 16 when it comes to the best place to be born (Australia, which was home for the first twenty-one years of my life, is number 2).

Interesting stuff, but let's get real. Let's talk about money, the stuff we use every day to pay for everything we need in Maslow's first level of needs. Two out of three American adults "lack financial literacy," according to the FINRA Investor Education Foundation, and only 37 percent would pass if required to take a basic financial knowledge test.

But we are only just getting started. Eighteen percent of respondents spend more than they earn; 21 percent have overdue medical bills; 26 percent have used non-bank borrowing (such as high-interest payday loans or pawn shop loans); 32 percent pay only the minimum due on their credit cards; and 9 percent are underwater on their home mortgages.

These are adults. The average twenty-one-year-old wouldn't know how to put together a personal budget if his life depended on it, but probably already has three or four credit cards, and more than 40 percent of them have signed up for a staggering amount of student debt that they neither understand nor know how they will pay off. And I am not convinced that the average forty-year-old knows much more.

So, we don't teach them about money. Nor do we teach them about relationships. How many twenty-one-year-olds do you think know how to resolve a conflict in a rational, mature way? What percentage do you think have been taught a simple process for conflict resolution, considering that conflict is inevitable in every relationship both personally and professionally? I don't know the answer; the number is so small that no researcher has considered it worth her time to do the work and find out.

We are failing our young people. As you are probably gathering, I could write a whole book about this, but the point is our education system doesn't need a tweak, it needs a complete overhaul. And it is corporate America that should stand up (with their army of lobbyists) and demand it. Why? Simple: because they are footing the bill. What's the number one cause of stress in a marriage or relationship? Money. What's the number one cause of workplace accidents? Stress. These are just two of a thousand connections between life skills and productivity at work.

It would be another book unto itself, but we also have to ask: Where are parents in all of this? But a parent who has not been taught about personal finances cannot teach his or her children about personal finances, and so the cycle perpetuates itself.

So, what does all this teach us? Two things: First, our education system needs to be completely overhauled. You and I both know that won't happen, so we'd better start looking for plan B. Second, the way we onboard and educate employees needs massive change to compensate for these inadequacies.

2. It may seem like a fairly simple and reasonable statement to say everything your employees do helps your organization become either the-best-version-of-itself or a-lesser-version-of-itself, but most people haven't yet considered the full implications of what it means for their organization. So, let's have a look at an example.

Robert holds a mid-level role at ABC Industries. One night he goes home from work and, having had a long day, decides he needs to relax a little. So, he plants himself in his huge recliner, in front of his 127-inch idiot box, with a six-pack of beer and a three-hundred-ounce bag of potato chips. An hour later he decides it's time for dinner, so he picks up the phone and orders two extra-large pizzas, with extra meat and cheese; two hundred-ounce bottles of Coke (one Diet, of course); two tubs of ice cream; and some chicken wings. He spends the rest of the night feasting like a modern king, but what is the result?

First, he will become a-lesser-version-of-himself. I mean, he will become a bigger version of himself, but in every way that really matters he will become a-lesser-version-of-himself. And in that moment ABC Industries becomes a-lesser-version-of-itself.

Whoa! Hold on a minute. The universe just shifted. Our modern, secular, relativistic culture objects, saying, "No. What Robert did was a personal act. It took place in the privacy and comfort of his very own living room. He was the only person there, and therefore is the only person affected by his actions." Wrong. Worse than wrong, it's insanity. But we will come back to that.

Robert's coworker Angela has had a tough day at work too. When she gets home all she wants to do is lie in front of the television and relax, but she doesn't. She gets changed, puts on her running shoes, and goes for a run.

While Angela is out running she is becoming a-better-version-of-herself. She is becoming a better friend, a better sister, a better daughter, and believe it or not, a better employee of ABC Industries. And while Angela is out taking that run, ABC Industries is becoming a-better-version-of-itself.

Our culture will once again object, claiming that what Angela did was a personal act. But nothing could be further from the truth. There is no such thing as a personal act. Everything we do, every day, affects everyone everywhere—and it affects those closest to us the most. For example, the way Robert spent his evening impacts how much money Angela will make next year. I know, this is crazy stuff, but it's true. It is the scariest idea in modern business.

For six hundred years we have been trying to separate the personal from the professional. We cannot. It is impossible. A lazy farmer dies of hunger. There is a direct connection between his work and the fruit of his work, or lack thereof. Whether you put fifty, a hundred, or even ten thousand people together in an office and call it an organization, the principle remains the same. Our personal actions affect our professional outcomes, not just individually but communally.

Hopefully you are starting to get the point, because now it's time to really blow your mind. Who is the craziest person on your team or in your organization? Next, who is the person in your organization who seems pretty normal but for whatever reason is currently doing something outrageously stupid in his life? Everything these people do and everything you do every day, personally and professionally, impacts your pay and benefits package next year. Everything. And we haven't even taken a look at some of the lazy, self-sabotaging things you do—and I've got my own stuff too.

Now, there will always be someone who says, "But Hemingway did his best work when he was drunk!" First, that isn't true. Despite popular myth, he never drank while he was working, but rather rewarded himself with alcohol after he had finished his allotted work for the day. Second, you're probably not the next Hemingway. Finally, he battled with misery and depression almost every day of his life before killing himself at age sixty-one. So he's probably not the best example.

So, what's the impact of this idea? Massive. You could put together a top-flight team of amazing researchers and it would take them more than a year to work out just the financial impact. So, let's use a simple example:

Imagine you begin working in a good culture at the age of 25 and work there your whole career, until age 65. And let's assume your annual pay raise over that time was 3 percent each year after starting *at $40,000. At 65 you will be earning $130,481.51 at a reasonably healthy organization. Now let's assume you work at a dynamic organization with a very healthy culture, remembering there is a direct connection between the health of a culture and profits. Instead of a 3 percent annual raise, you get 1.5 percent more on average, or a 4.5 percent annual increase. At age 65 you will be earning $232,654.58. That is a 78 percent difference.*

This simple illustration is just one tiny example of the personal impact a Dynamic Culture has on real people's real lives. If personal behavior has the same impact as culture, then just double all the numbers above and now we are looking at a 156 percent difference in compensation alone. But you and I both know there are a dozen other things that can be measured, and dozens more that can't be measured, that impact the quality of both our personal and professional lives. But the bottom line is, regardless of our role in the organization, we owe it to each other to build a phenomenal culture.

Warning: What I am about to share might be the most frightening idea in business today.

An employee with a highly functioning personal life is a better asset to your organization than an employee with a massively dysfunctional life.

Now, before anyone gets all defensive, it is important to point out that we all have dysfunction in our personal lives. Sometimes this takes the form of a constant low-level dysfunction, but it may also come unexpectedly as an all-consuming personal problem. The latter usually has an end date, and the former is usually manageable and rarely a huge distraction to a person's work.

But the incidence and level of dysfunction in people's lives is increasing. Have you noticed how quickly the world has changed over the past twenty years? Are there any signs that the change is slowing down? Is all the change good? No. So let's not be naive in thinking the change is slowing down anytime soon, or that the change is not going to continue to make people's lives more dysfunctional.

Team members cannot check their personal lives at the door like a coat when they arrive at work. Their work is impacted by their personal lives. That's why employees with highly functioning personal lives are a better asset to the organization than those with massively dysfunctional personal lives. It is also why organizations should invest in helping their people develop the skills necessary to thrive in their personal lives. That may mean hosting relationship courses, personal finance seminars, or health and well-being trainings.

The reverse is also true. Team members cannot check their work at the door when they go home. So we have a responsibility to foster a healthy environment by making their work as fulfilling as possible, but even more so, by treating people like people and doing everything possible to ensure that each new person is a positive addition to the team and culture.

The bottom line is that people who are happy in their personal lives tend be happier at work, and as a result tend to be more focused, have more energy, work harder, and be more productive. People who are unhappy in their personal lives (whether that lasts for a day, a month, or a decade) tend to operate in survival mode, getting done only what absolutely needs to be done. We shouldn't be surprised. We all experience this type of survival mode when we get sick. Even a common cold robs us of our focus, energy, and ability to work hard, and causes a massive drop in our productivity.

Now, let me ask you a question: Is the average person's life becoming more or less dysfunctional? More, right? Scary. I know it may not be very politically correct to say, but it just turns out to be the truth. A highly functioning employee with a highly functioning personal life is becoming an endangered species. If you are trying to accomplish anything, gathering a group of people who are healthy and happy in their personal lives increases your chances of success tenfold, perhaps more.

But your corporate lawyers and human resources department are starting to get pretty nervous about this idea and its implications. Because, let's be honest, you can't just sit down with prospective employees and say, "Tell me about all the dysfunctional things happening in your personal life at the moment."

It is also essential to remember that we all have some dysfunction in our lives. It may change from year to year, or decade to decade, but it's there. The point is not that some people have dysfunctional lives and others don't. We all have dysfunction in our lives, but some people have an awful lot more than others.

To be clear, I am not saying we should not hire such people. What I am saying is that we need to accept that the education system and society in general have not helped the average person to establish a highly functioning personal life. As a result, if we want to succeed, every organization needs to rethink its onboarding and training programs. These programs need to offer a lot more content that helps people develop life skills. We may think people should be doing these things for themselves, but this is a stale excuse and is clearly not going to happen.

Some will protest that these things are not a corporation's responsibility. Others have said to me, "This sounds like a form of corporate social work." Still others will add, "Where is personal responsibility in all of this?" I don't disagree, but society is what it is and the workforce is what it is, and so, in order for our organizations to succeed, we need to face these realities and improve them, not ignore them.

We are entering a new era of corporate training. We need to.

The Positive-to-Negative Ratio

People often ask me, "How can you speak to a group of Fortune 500 CEOs, a high school student body, a church community, a second-grade class, a group of politicians and community leaders, and an NFL team in the same week—and captivate each group in different ways?" The answer is really quite simple. I'm an observer of people. Half the things I write about are things you have already thought about. The message resonates because I have the gift of articulating what people already know to be true, and demonstrating how those insights can be put into practice. For my whole life, I have been observing myself and others. I know people. Describe a situation and I can probably tell you how 90 percent of people will respond. My craft is to know people. My worldview and philosophy are predominantly influenced by observation. My speaking and writing are just the ways of expressing that craft.

And people are people are people. Sure, some are educated and others are not; some are rich and others are poor; some come from loving families and others don't; some are driven and motivated and others are lazy and disoriented; and they all have different hopes, dreams, and visions for their lives. At the same time, we are remarkably similar in many ways. That is the human paradox: We are marvelously unique and astoundingly similar at once.

Psychologists John and Julie Gottman are experts in the

field of marriage and relationships. They can predict within fifteen minutes and with 94 percent accuracy if a couple will stay married or divorce. John created what has been dubbed the Love Lab, a couples laboratory set up like an apartment, with cameras that allow researchers to observe the couple. The couple usually spends twenty-four hours in the Love Lab, and a lot can be learned in that twenty-four hours, but the prediction is made after fifteen minutes.

When I first heard about this, I was absolutely fascinated. And of course, as someone keenly interested in observing human behavior, I wondered how they were able to do it. What do they watch for? What criteria do they base their predictions on? How often do they disagree with each other, and who has the tie-breaking vote?

But it turns out they rely on just one indicator, one measure: the relationship between positive and negative interactions. They call it the magic ratio, which is the Positive Negative Ratio (PNR).

Couples with a positive-to-negative ratio of 5:1 in a fifteen-minute interaction are likely to stay together. That's right, five positive interactions to one negative. Most people live in a mind space that thinks one positive action balances out one negative. Even more foolishly, we sometimes allow ourselves to believe that one positive action *cancels out* a negative action. Not so. Not even close. In fact, nothing could be further from the truth. You need five positive actions or interactions to even have a chance of making up for one negative event.

What does this have to do with corporate culture? PNR impacts everything. Put it in the context of your business. Let's say you are in the restaurant business. A customer has a bad experience. You send the manager over to apologize and she offers the disgruntled guest free dessert to sweeten the deal (literally). It's a good start, but that customer needs to have four more positive experiences at your restaurant just to balance out that one bad experience. And if it was his twenty-fifth wedding anniversary or his daughter's sixteenth birthday party, that number just multiplied.

Think about how important PNR is when it comes to brand. A brand is a promise, and great brands keep their promise. How many times does a person have to lie to you before you characterize that person as a liar? If someone has a negative encounter with your brand, it can take years to win her back; in fact, it's more likely you'll never win her back.

When it comes to the business aspects of our organizations, we are crystal clear about these things. So why do we struggle so much when it comes to applying these same principles to growing and managing our people?

Your organization is a community, which has a culture that is made up of many relationships. How many relationships do you have in your organization? Most people have a lot more than they realize when they really examine it. To establish a positive relationship with a colleague, you need a positive-to-negative ratio of at least 3:1. If you do something to really upset a colleague, you need to do five positive things to even have a chance of redeeming your personal brand with that person. If you are the CEO and you create a negative experience for your leadership team, you can see the implications; if you do something that is received negatively across the entire organization . . . well, you see what I am getting at. The PNR is something for all of us to be mindful of when we are interacting with others, and all it takes is a little intentionality to ensure a positive interaction.

An organization is made up of dozens, hundreds, or even thousands of relationships, and its culture is a collection of all those relationships. Every relationship is either positive or negative. Every encounter with another person usually leans positive or negative. Some may argue that interactions can also be neutral. But be honest, do you go on a second date with a person if the first one was just neutral? Probably not. And do you want your customers having a neutral experience with your products, services, and brand?

The multiplication of the positive-to-negative ratio across an organization leads very quickly to determining if a culture is positive or negative, healthy or unhealthy, highly functioning or massively dysfunctional. The PNR acts as a litmus test in so many aspects of our lives that involve relationship. It is a quick and easy way for leaders to take the temperature of their relationships with their direct reports, both individually and collectively. So the concept has powerful applications both personally and professionally. It probably wouldn't be a bad idea to teach high school students that if you are dating someone and your positive-to-negative ratio sucks, that's probably not a good sign. We can all apply the PNR to our personal relationships, with our spouse or significant other, with our children, friends, and neighbors.

Dynamic Cultures have high positive-to-negative ratios, and Culture Advocates intentionally try to create a positive experience in every interaction with a customer or colleague.

Culture Is Determined by Values

All organizations begin for a reason, to serve a particular need, and to fulfill a specific vision. They may grow more complex and explore other opportunities over time, but usually the original vision will live on in the culture forever. This is why when you really start to explore a culture, you usually have a few encounters with the founder's personality (or his or her ghost if he or she is no longer with us).

During his or her lifetime, the founder remains the guardian of the vision and the keeper of the dream. But once that person (or people) is no longer involved on a day-to-day basis, the original values and vision can be quickly lost. But the founder's fingerprints will still be all over the culture—and this is usually both a good thing and a bad thing. An organization's mission is derived from the founder's values and vision. We will explore the role of mission in depth in chapter three. For now, it is enough to note that having a clear mission and vision is essential to organizational health and Dynamic Culture.

Nothing will influence the PNR like values. Mission, vision, and values are the foundation upon which we build a successful organization and a Dynamic Culture. Values are what animate the culture every day. That word, *animate*, is really important to our conversation. It comes from the Latin word *anima*, which means "breath," "soul," or more literally, "to bring to life." Values breathe life into an organization; they give it a soul. Without values an organization becomes soulless, lifeless. A culture with no values at all isn't unhealthy; it is actually dead.

Every situation, every decision, every project raises questions. If an organization has clearly established mission and values and has explicitly and repeatedly communicated them to its employees—meaning they are well understood at all levels in the organization—these questions tend to be relatively easy to answer, and many of them can be answered at every level of an organization. But very few organizations have this kind of clarity; I would say less than 1 percent.

One of the simplest ways to differentiate a highly functioning organization from a poorly functioning organization is to observe their decision-making process. In the unhealthiest organizations, the answer to every question is: "Let me ask my boss." You explain your situation to your boss and she says: "Let me ask my boss," and so on. We have all experienced this frustration with some of the worst organizations in the world. In a Dynamic Culture, most of the decisions that emerge each day can be made quickly and in the most efficient and expeditious way possible, which means people at relatively low levels of the organization can make those decisions. In a really healthy culture, people other than the bosses can answer questions and make decisions.

Most of the time corporate values are a joke. They are decided by nobody knows who and in a room nobody knows where, and they have nothing to do with the reality of the day-to-day activities of the actual organization. They are aspirational at best. They get plastered on a wall at the head office and printed in corporate brochures, but the employees snicker at them; they consider the values a joke because they don't reflect the way people have been treated as team members and they don't reflect the way they see the organization treating customers each day. When your values are considered a joke, you have a very sick culture.

If you want to build a truly Dynamic Culture, get very clear about your values, start living them rigorously, and take every opportunity to briefly speak to team members and clients about them. You don't instill values in an organization by putting them on a sign. You instill values by coaching your people to live them—though the very best way is to hire people who already share your values.

Organizations that establish and practice their values have a massive advantage over their competitors. One of the most practical ways corporate values benefit a business is in the area of decision-making. The speed at which decisions get made within an organization is a leading indicator of cultural health. Clarity around our values massively accelerates the decision-making process—and to repeat myself because it warrants it, the lower down the organizational structure a decision can be made, the more healthy an organization is; this is a leading indicator.

But less than 1 percent of organizations have value clarity. My partners and I at FLOYD Consulting have worked with more than fifty Fortune 500 organizations and hundreds of small and medium-size businesses and organizations. When it comes to values clarity, the best I have seen is an organization based in Texas called the Dwyer Group.

The following is the Dwyer Group's Code of Values, which you can read more about in Dina Dwyer-Owens' book, *Values, Inc.* As you read through them, keep in mind that every Dwyer Group meeting begins with the recitation of the Code of Values, whether that meeting consists of two people or the whole organization. I have been at meetings where whoever is leading it begins by listing the first value and then each value is recited by a different team member in the meeting. They aren't reading from note cards—they know it by heart.

The Dwyer Group Code of Values

We live our Code of Values by . . .

Respect

. . . *treating others as we would like to be treated*

. . . *listening with the intent to understand what is being said and acknowledging that what is said is important to the speaker*

. . . *responding in a timely fashion*

. . . *speaking calmly and respectfully, without profanity or sarcasm*

. . . *acknowledging everyone as right from their own perspective*

Integrity

. . . *making only agreements we are willing, able, and intend to keep*

. . . *communicating any potentially broken agreements at the first appropriate opportunity to all parties concerned*

. . . *looking to the system for correction and proposing all possible solutions if something is not working*

. . . *operating in a responsible manner, "above the line . . ."*

. . . *communicating honestly and with purpose*

. . . *asking clarifying questions if we disagree or do not understand*

. . . *never saying anything about anyone that we would not say to him or her*

Customer Focus

. . . *continuously striving to maximize internal and external customer loyalty*

. . . *making our best efforts to understand and appreciate the customer's needs in every situation*

Having Fun in the Process!

How does your organization measure up to the Dwyer Group's Code of Values? How would your culture be different if these were your organizational values?

To learn more about Dina and the Dwyer Group, visit DinaDwyerOwens.com and DwyerGroup.com.

Values are the foundation of a great culture. Identify them—and don't be vague. Get specific about how they are lived out in different daily situations that you face at work. People increasingly want more than just money in return for their work. They want to work for an organization that has strong values and a great culture. Culture is an external expression of an internal reality. Values are that internal reality.

You don't instill values by printing signs and posting them all around the organization. You instill values by coaching your people to live them. But the best way of all, as we will soon discover, is to hire people who already have and respect your values.

Human beings have a powerful desire to belong. But more than simply belonging, we want to belong to something that we can be proud of and take joy in, and when we do, we tell everyone we know about it. Do your people feel like they belong in your organization? Do they feel that their contribution is valued? Do they take joy in telling others about where they work?

This is the root of why everyone wants to belong to a Dynamic Culture at work. We have begun to explore the challenges, problems, and opportunities of building a Dynamic Culture. Now let's venture into the culture solution.

2

why culture matters

Surprise and Delight

All great brands and products surprise and delight. Marketing professionals love surprise-and-delight campaigns. A marketing strategy that focuses on surprise and delight usually involves randomly selecting some customer to receive a free product or experience. But there is one thing that marketers salivate over even more than surprise-and-delight campaigns: products that actually surprise and delight.

Not long ago, I was meeting with a friend who talks about his car every time I see him. About two years ago he bought his first luxury car, and ever since, he has been evangelizing to everyone who will listen about the features, comfort, and performance of this car. It is clearly a surprise-and-delight product.

When I was leaving, I joked to his assistant, "Do you get sick of hearing about that car?" She smiled in a way that told me she was having a secret thought. I asked her what she was thinking, and she told me, "Well, I have to say, I do wish I had one. The other day I took it to the dealership for its regular service and oil change. They are amazing. It's not even my car, but they treated me like a princess. Coffee, magazines, food and snacks; they offered me a quiet place to work; the personal attention never ended." Wow. I walked away thinking, there is a brand that has combined a surprise-and-delight product with surprise-and-delight service.

But don't fall into the trap of thinking that a surprise-and-delight product has to be expensive. It has nothing to do with price. Ask people about their favorite fried chicken and you will see the look of surprise and delight in their eyes as they tell you why no other brand of fried chicken compares to their favorite. Ask mothers of young children about their favorite baby stuff and every single one of them will become animated as they tell you about some fabulous little thing that makes their lives so much easier. They have a disproportionate amount of appreciation for the object, whatever it is. There it is again: surprise and delight.

The surprise-and-delight factor is essential to every great product and service. Consider Amazon Prime—people are surprised and delighted by it. It started out as just free two-day shipping on all your orders (although *just* doesn't seem like the right word). But today it includes a hundred perks, including access to free music, movies, television shows, and e-books. Different people love Amazon Prime for different reasons, but surprise and delight is at the core of its success. This is a huge example and something most organizations could not replicate, but don't let that distract you. Whatever it is you do, whatever product or service you offer, you can surprise and delight your customers.

The guy in the car shop delights in the wrench that makes his role a little easier and a lot more enjoyable. The mother delights in the diaper that makes it easier for her to change her baby's diaper with one hand tied behind her back (figuratively, of course). Chocolate lovers delight in that sprinkle of sea salt atop the caramel that completely changes the experience.

What products or services continue to surprise and delight you over and over again? We all have favorites, and if you delve into why you enjoy them so much, you will find that they surprise and delight you.

A Dynamic Culture surprises and delights in a similar way. At first people delight in experiencing such a culture, and over time they delight in telling others about it. Everyone boasts about being associated with an organization that has a great culture. And if you ask them to tell you about the organization, they won't talk about the products and services. They won't talk about market penetration and geographic footprint. They will talk about the people and culture of that organization.

What's Your Most Important Product or Service?

Every day you have a chance to surprise and delight your customers with your products and services. The very good news is that they won't keep their surprise and delight to themselves. They will delight in telling others about it.

You may of course be wondering what all this has to do with culture. Let's take a look, but first, one more question: What is your organization's most important product or service?

When I ask this question I usually get answers like these:

"It's hard to say. Maybe Pampers—I mean, if it were its own organization it would be on the Fortune 500 list on its own.

But maybe it's Tide, which I think was our first billion-dollar brand."

"The iPhone. There's no doubt. We are popping up new billion-dollar organizations here and there, but people just yawn. It's going to be all about the iPhone for a long time, I suspect."

"Classic Coca-Cola. It's been the biggest-selling soft drink for, wow, I don't even know how many years. But I could see a future where our most important product is Dasani water."

"Life insurance. Everybody needs it. Everybody is always going to need it."

But I'd like to propose that your organization's most important product or service is its culture. I know, when investment bankers look at an organization's portfolio of products, they don't consider its culture. But they should.

Your culture is a product. It's also a service. Your employees and customers are consumers of your culture. Even though you and they may have never thought of it as a product, they consume it like they do other products and services every day—and they respond to it. Now, they may respond with surprise and delight, but they may also be responding with disdain or resentment. Most organizations don't know, because culture is the only product that they don't get customer feedback on. Many organizations will say, "But we do our annual engagement survey for employees." This is good and it has its place, but let's agree that if your culture were a billion-dollar brand you would be doing more.

The other piece that employee engagement surveys completely ignore is that customers don't get to participate, and they too are consumers of your culture. In fact, very often they have a much more clear-eyed vision of what your culture is really like than your employees do. I don't know a single organization that asks its customers about the organization's culture. We ask customers about service and their experience in general, but I wonder what they notice about the culture than we don't.

Your culture is your organization's most important product or service, but who is in charge of it? Who is responsible for ensuring its success? When was the last time you consulted someone on culture? When was the last time you benchmarked your culture against best practices? Do you know what's working and what's not working? The truth is, we wouldn't ignore products and services that are essential to the success of our business, but that's exactly what we do when we ignore culture.

I know. I know. You may already be thinking that your culture is so far away from being a surprise-and-delight culture that you doubt it is even possible. Or you may be thinking this is going to cost too much money, and that management and finance will never sign off on it. Think again.

There are lots of reasons we ignore culture, and we will deal with them all as we make our way through this book. But let's get the first three objections out of the way immediately.

1. Our culture is anything but a surprise-and-delight culture. There is no way we could ever build a Dynamic Culture. It is impossible.
2. We don't have the money to make our culture great.
3. I cannot ask any more of my people. They are already overworked.

Here are my responses:

1. It does not matter how dysfunctional your culture is; you can improve it massively with a plan and intentional

effort. Not only can we, but we must. People spend most of their lives working, and anything we can do to improve that experience is a moral imperative. You may not be able to create the best culture in the world, but you will be surprised how much you are able to improve a culture with consistent effort. Don't let what you can't do interfere with what you can do.

2. You don't need any money to start building a Dynamic Culture today. I know that seems hard to believe, but I'd ask you just to delay judgment for a few chapters and let me prove it to you.

3. The plan I will present does not require your people— leaders, managers, or employees—to do more than they are already doing. It may require them to do those things they are already doing differently and better, and it may require them to stop doing some things that are ineffective and replace them with more effective ways of doing things—better systems, processes, and behaviors, and clearer priorities—but their net workload will not increase. In fact, it may very well decrease, and it will certainly become more enjoyable. It takes more energy to maintain mediocrity than it does to pursue excellence.

Great culture is possible. What makes me so certain of this is that almost every employee wants to work in a great culture, and almost every leader wants to lead a great culture. And as radical as it may sound, people deserve a great culture that encourages them to do their best work, regardless of what that work is, and everybody is responsible and has a role to play in creating that culture.

Great Cultures Surprise and Delight

All great products, services, and experiences surprise and delight. From Disney to the Super Bowl, surprise and delight are essential to success. Great cultures surprise and delight too, though perhaps not in the ways you might think.

We usually only hear about corporate culture in the media when some massive tech organization makes a ridiculous benefit available to its employees such as sleep pods, unlimited vacation, or two years' maternity leave. I read recently about an organization that spends a million dollars a month on food for its employees. This kind of nonsense makes Dynamic Culture seem impossible for most organizations.

The average organization cannot replicate these, and so many have simply disengaged from the culture discussion altogether. But these headline-catching benefits are not culture. They might surprise and delight, but they might also be entitlement creators instead of empowerment builders.

An authentic culture creates empowerment; it doesn't build entitlement. This principle provides another very quick litmus test as your organization sets out to create a Dynamic Culture: Is what is being proposed more likely to lead to empowerment or to entitlement? Another great litmus test is to ask: How will people respond if whatever is being proposed is taken away at some point in the future?

For example, many years ago a team member at an organization I was leading suggested that we implement casual Friday and allow people to wear jeans or more comfortable attire than their regular business attire. It seemed harmless, so I agreed. Three years later, I noticed that due to some changes in our operations, more than 70 percent of our visitors came to our offices on a Friday before weekend programs we were offering. For this reason, I announced we were eliminating casual Friday in order to look and be at our best for our visiting clients. Were people disgruntled? No—I wish they were disgruntled. Their response was a disgrace. It had nothing to do with mission and everything to do with personal preference. But it is a very simple example of how quickly things can go wrong when we are making cultural decisions based on the wrong criteria.

There is a difference between a surprise-and-delight campaign and a surprise-and-delight product. When it comes to culture, a surprise-and-delight campaign is a very, very dangerous thing that will leave you worse off than when you started. Many organizations set out to build a great culture, but rather than building a great culture that genuinely surprises and delights on a consistent basis because it is based on values and substance, they do a surprise-and-delight campaign based on perks, which is unsustainable and sooner or later fizzles.

We will discuss what culture is and what it is not in more detail in the coming pages. But the truth is that a great culture is much more rudimentary than most people think. It's not about bringing your dog to work and nap pods. These are perks, not culture. They are at best very small aspects of culture, and much smaller than most would be led to believe.

So, what is the secret of a great culture? What idea, benefit, or opportunity do we find at the core of Dynamic Cultures? This might surprise you:

Treat people like people.

That's the secret to a Dynamic Culture. I know, it may seem anticlimactic, but it is the core value of great cultures. Treat your people like people and they will treat your customers like people, and you will create a great culture and be phenomenally successful.

I don't know what it says about society that simply treating people like human beings instead of like objects, sales, customers, results, profits, growth, or opportunities produces astounding levels of surprise and delight. The bar has been set so low that all you have to do to surprise and delight is treat people like people. I am not saying we should start there, but there are a great many situations in business in which it is incredibly difficult just to treat people like people. Have a little humanity. After all, how do you want them to treat your customers? Your employees are unlikely to treat your customers any better than you treat them.

If you really want to surprise and delight your employees, care about them more than any other organization on the planet does. Not blindly, because that will lead to abuse and entitlement. But there are written and unwritten contracts between employees and employers. You have expectations of your team that are not written down anywhere, like showing up to work and making their best efforts to fulfill their role and make the organization more successful. But if you treat people with dignity and respect, they will rise up in ways you never imagined.

How exactly do you accomplish this in the workplace? There are a hundred simple ways, and you know them, because they are how you like to be treated. But there is something else. Engage their genius. I promise you every person who works with you is a genius at something. Even if they can spend only 5 percent of their time working in their genius, it will animate the other 95 percent of their working time. It may animate their whole lives. Find their genius and give them an outlet for it.

Sometimes the best way to test a thesis is to explore the opposite. If it was your mission to destroy a culture, what would be the quickest way? Disrespect people. Disrespecting your employees and customers is the easiest way to poison a culture.

The easiest way to drive the idea of treating people like people deep into your culture is to stop pretending you have employees. There is no such thing. The people you call employees are actually your first customers. They will give you more than your biggest secondary customers (the people who buy your goods and services) ever will. These people you call employees—your first customers—give you their time, their health, their creativity, and their innovation; they sacrifice time with the people they love; and they give you their professional lives. They are your primary customers. Disrespect them and you will poison your culture.

In the pages that follow, you will learn how to create a surprise-and-delight culture simply by doing what you already do—better. You can create a surprise-and-delight culture without spending more money. In fact, creating such a culture will make you money in a hundred ways. I am not, however, saying that you should not spend money to create a truly Dynamic Culture, because I do think it is something worth investing in, and I have seen huge ROI on such investments. All I am saying is that you can get started without a penny—today!

How are we going to accomplish all these miracles? Again: *Treat people like people.* Respect is the currency of great cultures.

If you really want to surprise and delight people, don't treat them like employees or customers—treat them like people. Surprise people by caring about them more than any other organization on the planet does. In response, they will give you an incredible culture, fierce loyalty, and phenomenal results, to name but a few.

Organizations that do not surprise and delight their employees are unlikely to surprise and delight their customers. It is unreasonable to expect your employees to behave differently toward your customers than you behave toward your employees. Treat your employees and customers like human beings. That's how you develop a culture that creates unmatched profitability and sustainability.

Like all great products and services, a culture should delight. Does your culture delight your employees and customers?

How Much Does Culture Matter?

It matters more than you think. You can never take it too seriously. Sure, everyone says it is important, but few organizations spend time or money specifically focused on improving their culture, and in 99 percent of organizations nobody is responsible for ensuring the culture is dynamic. Remember that a strong culture increases profits by 756 percent over a period of eleven years. So why isn't it someone's role to ensure that your culture becomes more dynamic every year?

"This culture stuff," as I recently heard a leader refer to it, really matters. It matters more than most people think, and it matters more with every passing year, because every new generation of workers places a higher priority on it than the generation before. It is actually of monumental importance; you can't exaggerate this importance in your organization's destiny. Ignore it at your peril and the peril of the organization you work with or lead.

Culture matters even more than those who think it matters a lot think it does. What I'm trying to say is, you can't exaggerate the importance of culture in your organization's destiny. It eats strategy for breakfast, but it eats sales and marketing for lunch, and new product development for dinner. And yet culture gets ignored in many of the most important organizational discussions each year.

The great majority of organizations massively underestimate the value of culture. Now, that is a very bold statement. Can I prove it with a mathematical equation or a longitudinal study from a well-respected research institute? No. But here's the thing: I have met many business leaders who thought culture was important, or even very important, but I have never met a business leader who overestimated how important culture was to the success of their organization.

Nothing matters more than culture in the long run. There are literally an unlimited number of reasons why this is true, and we will discuss many of them as we make our way through the six immutable principles of building a Dynamic Culture. But here are a few to whet your appetite.

- Culture is the difference between long-term, sustainable success and failure.
- Culture is the difference between a highly engaged workforce and a quit-and-stay workforce.
- Culture is the difference between happy team members and miserable team members.
- Great cultures change the conversation at every dinner table, when an employee's family asks: How was work today? And that conversation forms the way our children think about work, which is the earliest professional

development the next generation of team members at your organization and others receive.

- Dynamic Cultures add value in ways that are impossible to name or measure.
- A Dynamic Culture saves an organization from wasting resources on turnover, on attracting talent, and on training new employees—all of which distract your most talented people from your biggest opportunities. So it should be no surprise that great cultures lead to astounding profitability.
- Organizations literally live or die on culture.

The number one reason organizations underestimate the value of culture is something I have never heard spoken about in the corporate world. But to understand how important what I am about to say is, consider this question: If you were going to war, would you rather have a conscripted army (forced to work), a mercenary army (only doing it for the money or loot), or a volunteer army (fighting for something they believe in)?

It wouldn't matter whether I was leading the whole army or the lowest-ranking member of that army, I'd want it to be the last type, volunteer. A volunteer army would be more cohesive, more passionate, and more likely to take a personal risk to help me if I got into trouble, and they would be much more likely to win.

Now, I am not suggesting we all volunteer to do our work, but here's the thing most organizations never consider or discuss: How many hours a week do you think your employees collectively volunteer for your organization? I mean hours you don't *officially* pay them to work. Perhaps they arrive a bit early or leave a little late. Maybe they work after they get their children in bed to finish a project, catch up on email, or just plan the next day. They might take a short lunch, eat lunch at their desk, or occasionally miss lunch altogether, because they believe something is so important they are willing to freely make that sacrifice. Your organization doesn't pay them for any of this work.

This is corporate voluntarism, and it is huge—massive, actually. And yet, we never talk about it. When we discuss voluntarism, we typically speak about a team that went down to the local soup kitchen Friday night to help, or another team that visited the children's hospital. But the majority of volunteer hours freely given by your employees each year are given directly to your organization. And the quality of your culture directly determines the number of hours your people volunteer each year. It's fascinating—the better your culture is, the more likely people are to work way beyond what is officially required of them and what they are compensated for in dollars and cents.

The number one reason culture matters more than anything in the long run is because it ignites passion, and people who are passionate about something will do whatever it takes to win.

The Six Immutable Principles

A few weeks ago, someone asked me, "If you could do anything other than be a writer, what would you choose to do?" I didn't have to think about it; I have thought about it before: I'd be a musician. As a writer, I get to process life, ideas, and experiences through words. I love being a wordsmith for this and many other reasons. Musicians get to process the world through music, and music touches people on a soul level, in the same way and in different ways books do.

Did you know that music is made up of just twelve notes? Think about all your favorite songs and then consider the history of music in every genre: twelve notes.

Dynamic Cultures are made up of less than twelve notes. Half that many, in fact: just six. In the coming pages, instead of telling you a hundred things you should be doing in your organization to transform the culture, I'm going to teach you to do just six things, and I'll encourage you to do them with growing excellence. And I cannot tell you how excited I am to share them with you, and teach you how to drive them deep into the life of your organization and enjoy the fruits of a Dynamic Culture that you helped create.

The music of Dynamic Cultures is made up of six notes. Learn to play these six notes really well and your culture will become something to marvel at.

My preference would be to reveal them one at a time in the coming chapters, but something tells me that a bird's-eye view of the whole model from the outset may serve you better. So, here they are, the Six Immutable Principles of a Dynamic Culture:

Principle 1:   Make Culture a Priority
Principle 2:   Mission Is King
Principle 3:   Overcommunicate the Plan
Principle 4:   Hire with Rigorous Discipline
Principle 5:   Let People Know What You Expect
Principle 6:   Grow Your People by Creating a Coaching
                Culture

There they are. Building a Dynamic Culture is about mastering these six aspects of organizational life. The heart and soul of this book is about teaching you how to become an advocate for each of them, regardless of your role or position within the organization.

I labored over how exactly to describe the six principles, and finally settled on *immutable* after long and tiresome thought. Sometimes I think I torture myself unnecessarily over these things, but I always return to the fact that a wordsmith owes his or her readers just that kind of torture. Anyway, I chose the word *immutable* because it means "unchanging."

Many things will change about your organization's culture in the decades to come, but these six principles will remain. For years I have studied organizational culture and the cultures of thousands of organizations so that I could strip away everything that is fleeting, superficial, and transient, and the myriad of passing fads, in order to present you with the essence of culture and, more important, the very foundation upon which to build a Dynamic Culture.

Why is it so important to find the essence of culture? Because the essence of something is unchanging. For it is those things that are unchanging that allow us to make sense of change. So, at a time when change has never been more constant or intense, what is unchanging is more valuable than ever before. Wherever people gather for a common purpose, these six principles will hold their relevance.

People come up with dozens of ideas every month about how the culture of their organization could be improved. How do we decide which ideas to implement and which ideas not to implement? The quick and easy litmus test is to ask: Will this idea help this organization become a-better-version-of-itself? If the answer is no, then you need not waste any more time on it. If the answer is yes, the next question to ask ourselves is: Which of the six principles will it strengthen? If it does not find a home within one of the six immutable principles, then chances are it is a passing fad and should be treated as worse than a distraction.

The six principles are your North Star in your organization's journey to build an amazing culture. Would a sailor trade the North Star for a powerful spotlight that could easily break? Would a man of the sea trade the North Star for a fancy new untested navigational system? Nor should you trade these six principles—for anything!

As we have discussed, building a Dynamic Culture is about mastering these six principles of organizational life. I chose the word *mastering* with great intention also. What does it mean to master something? What does it take to master something like playing an instrument or a sport; marketing, public relations, or accounting; or something as simple and important as listening to people? What does it take to master the art of really listening to people?

The mastery of almost anything is about the basics. As human beings, we are fascinated with things that are new and different, special or extraordinary, the latest shiny, sparkly things. But almost all success and happiness in this world is born from ordinary things. We allow ourselves to be seduced by the spectacular, but the basics are where you find the true treasure. And it is just as easy for an organization and its culture to be seduced by things that are new and different and sparkly as it is for us as individuals.

When I first moved to the United States from Australia, I was fascinated by American football. I had grown up watching Australian football, rugby, and soccer. At first American football seemed like a foreign language. When something seems mysterious to you, there is a built-in bias to believe it is more complicated than it actually is. Don't get me wrong, American football is one of the most strategic sports in the world. But everything has its basics, and those basics are the key to success, the foundation of long-lasting excellence.

Through our consulting work my colleagues and I have had the opportunity to work with some NFL coaches, players, and teams, and one interaction with a head coach perfectly demonstrates what I am trying to share with you here.

MK: "Who do you think will win the Super Bowl this year?"

Coach: "Same team that won last year, and the year before that, and the year before that."

MK: "What do you mean? Three different teams have won the Super Bowl in the last three years."

Coach: "That's where you are wrong. That's where most players and most amateur coaches get it wrong too."

MK: "I'm not following you."

Coach: "The same team wins the Super Bowl every year."

MK: "What are you talking about? You sound like you've been drinking or we're in an episode of Abbott and Costello. Is this like a 'Who's on First?' thing?"

Coach: "No. I haven't been drinking. I mean every word I have said, and I am completely serious. The same team wins the Super Bowl every year: the team that has the discipline to master the basics. Football has a handful of basics. There are a thousand different plays, but they all rest on the offense and defense carrying out the basics of football with unerring consistency."

Success at almost anything rests upon this single principle: Do the basics, do them well, and do them every day, *especially when you don't feel like doing them*. It doesn't matter if it is football or any other sport, personal finances, physical fitness, marriage, parenting, military operations, small business, big business, or creating a dynamic organizational culture. This is one of the reasons most people don't become phenomenally successful. They lack the persistence to do the same things over and over, to focus on the smallest improvements in the most mundane parts of whatever it is they are doing. Success at almost anything is usually the result of being the very best at four or five things.

But we are so easily distracted by things other than the basics. After a big game in any sport, the journalists will be grilling the winning coach or player(s), trying to understand the secret to their success. The coach or player will say something like, "Well, the offense had a couple of opportunities and capitalized on them with discipline. And the defense executed the basics really well." Now, to the media and people watching at home, it can seem like the coach or player is being evasive and trying to keep the secrets of their success to themselves, but they aren't. They are actually being completely honest and transparent, but our love affair with the spectacular causes us to be disappointed that something so simple (not easy) could be the key to success.

Mastering the basics *is* the secret to success. So, as we make this journey together, resist the temptation to look beyond the basics of the six immutable principles of building a Dynamic Culture, and resist the seduction of the latest media about some corporate culture fad.

Culture Advocates focus on the basics. Dynamic Cultures make music with just six brilliant notes. Do these six things really, really well and you will build an astounding culture that attracts, grows, nurtures, and retains the very best people.

Throwing yourself into the basics day after day may get tedious from time to time, but success never gets tedious. At four a.m. when the Olympic athlete doesn't feel like getting out of bed—because, let's face it, nobody would—they envision themselves with that gold medal around their neck and the national anthem playing.

So yes, committing to the basics every day may occasionally get tiresome, but let me tell you what doesn't get old, ever: coming to work alongside other people you enjoy working with, and together passionately pursuing your mission. That can and should be fun—and incredibly fulfilling.

What Is Culture?

Culture is tremendously misunderstood. There is enormous confusion surrounding what is and what isn't culture, even among the highest level of organizational leaders today. This fire is constantly being stoked by the media with crazy stories about some insane perk some organization has decided to offer its employees, which is being touted as part of its great culture, when usually it has nothing to do with culture and the organization may or may not be around a year from now.

The first thing you learn from a media consultant is: Never

automatically accept the premise of a question. If you are asked, begin by questioning in your mind whatever the question assumes. I would like to encourage you to adopt a similar mind exercise anytime culture is mentioned at work, in the media, or in conversation. Start by asking which of the six principles it relates to—if you cannot easily connect it with one of the six principles we are about to discuss, there's a pretty good chance it has nothing to do with culture.

Anything that creates entitlement is either a fad or bad culture. Dynamic Cultures create empowerment, not entitlement.

One of the questions I ask leaders in our executive off-site retreats is: What is it about your organization that keeps you awake at night? Most of them joke that they are so tired by the time they do finally get to bed that nothing keeps them awake. The question, of course, is both literal and metaphorical.

Talk to any seasoned leader and they will tell you that the business of business is pretty straightforward. From time to time a marketing, finance, or supply chain situation might keep them awake at night. But that's the answer to the question only about 10 percent of the time. The other 90 percent of the time what weighs heavy on leaders' minds is people and culture. The two, not surprisingly, are inseparable.

When it comes to culture, there is a lot of confusion. What it is and what it isn't are the two main ideas at the center of that confusion. So, let's explore them together.

Culture is not just a collection of personal preferences. Too often we hear stories about people being able to bring their dogs to work; having unlimited vacation time; wearing anything they want to work; getting free snacks; being allowed to work from their local coffee shop instead of coming to the office; etc. These may masquerade as culture, but they are trifles.

In fact, many of these things can do more damage than good. And the misguided, misplaced, and recklessly irresponsible idea that they are at the core of a Dynamic Culture and that you cannot have a great culture without such perks is what causes many leaders and organizations to give up on culture improvement even before they have begun.

This book is not about those types of fleeting, empty, pretend cultures, because at best these perks are only very loosely related to culture. At worst, if one day you have to eliminate one of these perks for reasons that are valid, logical, and immensely reasonable, you will experience the wrath of entitlement at a level that is completely disproportionate to the situation at hand. This will of course massively damage morale and be considered a direct attack on the organization's culture. Thus, something that had virtually nothing to do with culture to begin with will end up doing real damage to your organization's actual culture.

So, let's be clear from the start: The goal of a Dynamic Culture is not to make employees happy. The best an organization can do is create an environment where it is possible for employees to establish happiness for themselves. A Dynamic Culture cannot make employees happy, but it can make fulfillment and happiness at work a lot more attainable.

Here's the problem. While an organization cannot make employees happy, it can make them miserable. The number one complaint of employees is their manager. I don't care how good your personal life is or how positive your attitude is, a bad manager can make you and your life very miserable. And this is just one example of how an unhealthy culture can make people unhappy.

While we are talking about managers, I'd like to propose that we eradicate the term *manager* from organizational life. Who wants a manager? Who wants to be *managed?* Wouldn't everyone prefer a leader? Why can't a team manager be a team leader? Can a shift manager be a shift leader? Would you rather introduce the person you report to as, "This is my manager, Jacqueline," or "This is my team leader, Jacqueline"?

I understand we all need direction and accountability, and certainly the work of various people needs to be coordinated in order to accomplish the desired team outcome. Does it matter if we call the person a manager or a leader? Yes. Unless there is a really, really good reason to call someone a manager, I say we call him or her a leader.

How many people do you know who are miserable at work? It's a big number. I could quote the latest research, but it would be out of date before this book gets published, and you probably have a rough sense anyway. Another question: How many people do you know who would love to leave their current role or organization? Again, that's a big number. At least 40 percent of employees in the average culture are actively looking for another role with another organization.

Culture can change that. In fact, it might be the only thing that *can* change it in the long term. Turnover and disengagement have plagued organizations for decades. They are so expensive that if we were able to accurately measure their real cost, every serious leader of an organization would make it their number one priority to create a culture so dynamic that nobody would ever want to leave.

Now let's turn to the real question: *What is culture?*

Culture is the soul of an organization. You cannot necessarily see it or touch it, but it is always there. It influences everything that happens within an organization, from who gets hired and fired to how safe people feel presenting a new idea or pointing out a problem, how much people enjoy coming to work, and how effectively teams accomplish their work.

According to *The Business Dictionary*, "Organizational culture encompasses values and behaviors that contribute to the unique social and psychological environment of an organization." Really? I mean, maybe academically that's how they describe it, but I'm not sure how any business would set about practically applying it.

David Needle says, "Organizational culture represents the collective values, beliefs, and principles . . . and is the product of such factors as history, product, market, technology, strategy, type of employees, management style, and national culture." He goes on to assert that culture includes the organization's vision, values, norms, systems, symbols, language, assumptions, beliefs, and habits.

Want something even more complicated? Organizational development expert Edgar H. Schein writes, "Organizational culture is defined as a pattern of shared basic assumptions that a group learns as it solves its problems of external adaptation and internal integration, that have worked well enough to be considered valid, and therefore, to be taught to new members as the correct way to perceive, think, feel in relation to these problems." Mr. Schein may be a genius, I don't know, but this sounds more like a cult than a place I'd like to work.

These all seem disconnected from the people and organizations I encounter and love working with. Another thing that strikes me is that all three definitions are completely passive. Dynamic organizational cultures don't just happen—they are built. So, let's start again. What is culture?

It seems to me we should never think deeply about anything without first considering the purpose of that thing. The purpose of culture is to help an organization better fulfill its mission with the understanding that a healthy environment will best serve that mission in the long run. From that perspective, culture is everything an organization does that helps it become the-very-best-version-of-itself, and everything it does to fulfill its mission better this year than it did last year. If someone or something helps your organization become a-better-version-of-itself, embrace it. If someone or something prevents your organization from becoming a-better-version-of-itself, run.

But, but, but . . . it is very important to remember this single outrageous idea when we are discussing culture: We are here to work. I know it may seem like a blatant announcement of the obvious, but too often that reality gets thrown out the window when organizations start talking about culture. When we forget we are here to work, when we disconnect our discussions about culture from our individual work and collective mission, those conversations move quickly toward things that can actually be a real distraction from the work at hand. I know it may seem crazy, but when it comes to work, we are actually here to accomplish something.

It is impossible, therefore, to establish a Dynamic Culture without a clear sense of mission (principle two). Everything about any culture should help you accomplish your mission more effectively.

We may not be able to agree on a definition, but one thing everyone can agree on is that as an employee, you know when a culture is healthy and when it is unhealthy and dysfunctional. You know a Dynamic Culture when you see it and when you get to experience and enjoy it every day. And customers can tell too.

But for the sake of clarity, let's agree on a definition of culture to use as a reference point throughout the rest of this book:

Culture is the vision, values, systems, language, expectations, behaviors, and beliefs that increase or decrease an organization's chances of accomplishing its strategy and fulfilling its mission, which in turn increases or decreases how much people enjoy coming to work.

It might be a great exercise to break the definition down into practical examples in your organization. You may want to do it on your own, or you may want to do it as a team. *Warning: No culture is perfect, so don't just focus on the positives. I have set up questions to help with that.*

- What's the vision?
- What are the organization's values (good and bad, spoken and unspoken)?
- What are the systems that help you accomplish your mission? What systems get in the way of accomplishing your mission?
- What is some of the unique language used in the organization that helps people buy into the mission (or accomplish it)? What language is counterproductive?
- What is expected of you and your team?
- What behaviors increase or decrease the organization's chances of success?
- What beliefs are central to the vision and mission? How are they upheld and how are they violated?
- What increases and decreases how much you enjoy coming to work?

It is also imperative to recognize that culture is not static. It constantly changes for better or for worse. The thing to be very clear about is that if you don't have a vision of the culture you want for your organization and a plan to bring about that culture, a culture will emerge anyway—and sooner or later, that unintentional culture becomes a wild beast.

In many ways, culture is an ongoing conversation about who you are as an organization and who you want to become. Culture is not something you determine once and then it is done. There may be pieces of your culture that are unchanging and nonnegotiable—such as mission, vision, and values—but there may also be pieces of your organization's culture that change over time. If you have fifty employees and you grow to 250 employees, your culture is going to change—guaranteed. The only question is, are you going to envision and drive that new culture or just see what happens? I'd recommend the former.

The First Principle:
MAKE CULTURE A PRIORITY

The first of the six principles is: MAKE CULTURE A PRIORITY. This principle cannot exist on its own; in fact, together the six principles make up an ecosystem, with all of them dependent on one another for success.

On one hand, there is actually very little to know about the first principle, because if you activate the other five principles, the first one will thrive. On the other hand, if you announce that you are going to make your organization's culture a priority and then fail to follow through with the other five principles, you will look foolish and lose the trust of everyone you lead. So let's not allow that to happen.

But leader or not, you have a role to play in all six principles. And while we are on the topic of leadership, when it comes to Dynamic Culture, everyone leads.

Leadership is an interesting thing. I have seen the world—I know how difficult work and life are for millions of people, and I know life is messy. As a result, the older I get, the less I am certain about. But when it comes to leadership, I am certain of three things:

1. People are desperate for bold leadership. Not the timid, namby-pamby, politically correct crap that has begun to dominate the leadership landscape. People want their leaders to be bold and brave, and these qualities are contagious. If a leader doesn't possess them, you are unlikely to find them on the front lines.

2. You become a leader by leading, not because somebody comes up to you one day and says, "You're a leader; now, go off and lead!" As the owner of a business, if I see a piece of trash on the floor in the office, I pick it up. But I know a dozen other people walked past it. Is it a small thing? Tiny. But leadership is made up of a million of those tiny things. If you are waiting for someone to appoint you as the leader of something, stop it. Leadership isn't something someone gives you. You just wake up and start doing it. Speak up in meetings when you have something of value to add, make a decision when nobody can decide where to go for lunch . . . lead.

3. "But I don't know how to be a leader!" I often hear people say this, but it is not so. You have already taken the best leadership course available to any person: your own experience of leaders. The problem is you probably forgot

to take notes. The good news is you can go back and re-create those notes, because the class was so well taught. Get yourself a fresh notebook. I love those Moleskine journals. Buy yourself one; it will be one of the best investments you ever make in your career. Then spend a few hours re-creating the notes from the most important leadership class you will ever take. Make a list of all the leaders you have ever had in your life—good and bad, formal and informal. Everyone from your first boss to your parents, every teacher you ever had, your school principal, and your coaches for football, volleyball, baseball, and any other sport you ever played. Next, make an exhaustive list of all the good qualities these leaders displayed. Finally, make a list of all the negative or horrible things these leaders ever did. Then you are ready to lead. Do the things on the second list, and don't do the things on the third list. That's leadership, and that's life. We learn as we go.

The first mistake we make when it comes to creating a Dynamic Culture is *we don't believe it is possible.* There are very few organizations with really fabulous cultures out there, and the number one reason is because most organizations don't actually believe establishing a Dynamic Culture is possible. This is primarily because most people have no idea where to start when it comes to building a world-class organizational culture.

The second mistake most people make when it comes to establishing a vibrant culture at work is believing we can't do anything about it personally. Everyone has a role to play in creating a Dynamic Culture. It doesn't matter if you are a business owner, an executive, a team leader, or an individual contributor who works alone in a scary dark basement in the recesses of the corporate headquarters—you can and should be a Culture Advocate.

Sooner or later, every single person in any organization personally decides to advocate or abdicate culture. Advocate or abdicate? You decide. But please, if you decide to abdicate all responsibility for building a great culture, don't complain about the culture. Nobody likes people who complain about things but are not willing to help fix them. Don't abdicate your cultural power or responsibility, and however small, start doing something amazing today.

Culture advocacy isn't just a leadership thing. You don't have to be the CEO to be a Culture Advocate. In fact, you don't need to be a leader of any type—though you have a better chance of becoming CEO someday if you are a Culture Advocate. But whatever your role, in your own way, in your own place, in your own time, you can be a Culture Advocate, and becoming one will significantly increase your fulfillment and engagement at work, transform the trajectory of your career, and change the story of your life.

With this in mind, I wrote this book not just for leaders, but also for every person in your organization. Something that drives me crazy as a consultant (and as an author) is when all the leaders in an organization read a book but they don't share it with the people working on the front lines and in the trenches. Too many books are written just for leaders; as a result, the message never makes it all the way through the organization.

That's why I specifically set out to write this book for everyone in your organization. There will be parts that apply more to leaders, and there will be parts that apply more to people serving the organization in other ways. But I have tried to write those sections in a way that helps leaders understand the challenges faced each day by the people they lead, and at the same time helps everyone in the organization understand how difficult it is to lead. For any human relationship to thrive, each of us must put ourselves in the other person's shoes and consider what is happening from their perspective. This mutual understanding of each other's roles and challenges is essential to creating a Dynamic Culture.

Everyone has a role to play in creating a great culture where people love coming to work. Everybody is called to be a Culture Advocate. *A Culture Advocate is someone who is passionate about improving the culture they work in—and who does one thing every day to improve that culture.* Are you a Culture Advocate? It doesn't really matter right now. Maybe you are, and maybe you're not. But I do hope that by the time you get to the end of this book, I will have inspired you to become a Culture Advocate and taught you how to do it.

Everyone has a role to play in creating a Dynamic Culture, and everybody can and should become a Culture Advocate. But we human beings—you and me—are exceptional at coming up with excuses based on excellent nonsense to justify why we won't do something that we know we absolutely should do (and do really, really well).

The biggest lie when it comes to culture is: "Everything we do is about culture." This is the great generalist's excuse. It's not true and everybody knows it, but it's the reason nobody is in charge of overseeing culture in most organizations, and why there is no budget to improve it.

Then there is the "unique" excuse: "Our organization is different. So this stuff you are talking about doesn't really apply to us." The only way this monumental self-deception could be true is if your organization has no employees—in which case I am seriously questioning why you are reading this book.

Other common excuses used by culture abdicators include: "Our organization is just too big to do anything about the culture." "Our organization is too small for all that culture stuff." "We can't afford to have a Dynamic Culture." Actually, as we will soon discover, you can't afford *not* to have one.

Finally, there is the "individual" excuse: "It's not my job." Wrong. It's part of everyone's role and it is everyone's responsibility.

Before our time together comes to an end we will have abolished all these excuses and myths and replaced them with practical ways everyone in your organization can help build a Dynamic Culture, so that people will love coming to work and accomplishing great things together.

Everyone has a role to play in creating a Dynamic Culture. It doesn't matter what your position is in the organization. I have worked with receptionists who were phenomenal Culture Advocates, and I have met team leaders, janitors, and CEOs who were great Culture Advocates. Just start doing one thing every day to make the culture more dynamic. You don't need position, permission, or a budget to make new employees feel welcome. And this is just one of a thousand ways to improve your organization's culture. Visit CultureAdvocate.info and sign up for weekly tips for improving your culture.

Don't let what you can't do interfere with what you can do. What can you do today? A Culture Advocate does one thing every day to improve his or her organization's culture. Begin today. Become a Culture Advocate.

So where do we start?

A great place to begin is by assessing the current state of your culture. While we don't know if Peter Drucker said, "Culture eats strategy for breakfast," we do know he wrote, "What gets measured gets improved."

So, give your culture a score between 1 and 10 right now. Write it down in the margins of this page. Next, ask each member of your team to give the culture a score between 1 and 10. If you are the CEO, president, founder, or owner, ask every person in the organization to score the culture. 1 = soul-crushing, pathetic, miserable, and sick, get me out of here as soon as possible; 10 = dynamic, amazing, healthy, my friends are jealous of the culture here, and I never want to leave.

Now it is time to get busy improving your culture score. In the pages that follow you will find a plan to make your culture a place that nobody ever wants to leave.

What will be the biggest obstacle? Most people don't believe it is possible. If you are in a skeptical or, worse, a cynical state of mind about culture, all I ask is that you stay open to the idea that it's possible.

Right now, there are very few Dynamic Cultures out there, and as a result most businesses and too many leaders believe achieving this type of culture is not possible. I promise you, it is, and in the following pages I will show you exactly how to do it—not in theory, in practice.

Make culture your organization's moon shot. In 1961, when President John F. Kennedy announced that by the end of the decade the United States would land a man on the moon, he didn't know if we would or not. He hoped we would. It took almost a decade, and it is going to take several years to transform your organization into a Dynamic Culture. It won't take you a decade to transform your culture if you get serious about it, but it will make all the difference.

Will some people think you are crazy? Absolutely. When JFK announced to the world that we would go to the moon by the end of the decade, tons of people around the world and in his

own administration thought he was crazy. So yes, some people will think you are crazy, but that's OK.

Does your organization even have a goal for the next decade? A Dynamic Culture is a decade-worthy goal. It's the right thing to do. And sometimes, when all the debating and analyzing are over, all it really comes down to is that one question: Is it the right thing to do? Sometimes that alone is enough of a reason. In fact, that is always enough reason to do something big, bold, and now. We are not looking to put a man on the moon; we are looking to put humanity and dignity back into work. Human dignity—is that too much to ask?

Did you know you can turn lead into gold? Yep, that surprised me when I first heard it. I had to research it because I was skeptical of the idea, but it turns out to be true. Lead can be turned into gold—but not without fire. There needs to be heat for the transformation to occur. You can transform your culture, however ordinary, into a Dynamic Culture, but you'll need heat to make it happen.

Just let this one defining question guide you in every decision. It is the one question that always points out true north: Will what we are considering help our organization become the-best-version-of-itself? Allow this question to guide you and together you will develop a Dynamic Culture. A Dynamic Culture helps an organization become the-very-best-version-of-itself, become a desirable place to work, and exponentially increase its chance of success.

The First Principle:
MAKE CULTURE A PRIORITY

3

what matters most?

Protect Your King

I can't play chess. It's one of those things that have always been on my dream list but I have never gotten around to. No, that's not true. It's a lie, in fact, and it's amazing how often we lie to ourselves. It's not that I have never gotten around to it. I have just never made it a priority. Life is not a matter of "getting around to" things—we never do. We either make something a priority or we don't.

What we are about to discuss is indispensable to building and sustaining a Dynamic Culture. It is also indispensable to building and sustaining a successful business, nonprofit, or organization of any type.

Life is about choosing priorities and putting them at the center of our lives. We do this by passionately placing what matters most at the center of each day. How we live our days is how we live our lives; that is true for a person and for an organization. This is just one of the reasons why it is so very important that we know what matters most and what matters least.

But returning to our discussion of chess: The point is I know very little about it. Though there is one thing that I am very, very clear about when it comes to the game: I know it is crucial to protect your king. This is central to both surviving and winning. Chess coaches say things like: "Build a guard of pawns around your king early in every game." "Keep your king surrounded by these 'bodyguards' for the whole game if necessary, but certainly as long as possible." "Never move your king's guards unless your opponent forces you to."

Great players are constantly thinking of ways to protect and advance their king, and when it comes to the success of an organization, the very same principle is true. Everyone is responsible for protecting the king. Every move an organization makes, every policy or strategy should consider the implications that such a move will have on its king. But the ideal scenario is that every strategy advances the king.

As a result, one of the biggest questions that every organization needs to answer, clearly define, continually remind every team member of, and overcommunicate internally and externally is: Who or what is king of your organization?

Who Is the King?

Every organization has a king. In extremely unhealthy cultures, people don't know who or what is king from one day to the next. This leaves them guessing which way the wind is blowing on any given day, and wasting tons of time and energy lost in gossip and politics.

Who or what is king in your organization? The founder? The CEO? The customer? Which customer? Any customer or just some special customers? The owner? The owner's family members? The board? The union? The shareholders? The community? They cannot all be king. We have all met CEOs who thought they were the king or queen of that organization. It's arrogant and unattractive. Most family businesses have to deal with feuds between various family members—often as the second or third generation takes over the organization—many of whom wish to appoint themselves king.

Now, you might be wondering what on earth I'm talking about, and that's OK. So let me explain, because this really matters. *If you don't get this right, it is really hard to get anything else right around organizational clarity and culture.*

In the organizations I am involved in as the leader or the owner, there are two sayings that everyone is used to hearing a lot:

1. Mission Is King.
2. Matthew is not king!

The most effective way to serve everyone's best interests is to make mission king. Nothing trumps mission. What's the mission? What are we really trying to accomplish here above all else? If that is not the most important thing, the organization will be repeatedly kidnapped by egos, career climbers, whims, and fancies, and constantly be engaged in a massive game of organizational tug-of-war.

The Second Principle:
MISSION IS KING

Every organization needs an unchanging point of reference. This becomes the organization's North Star, building confidence on nights when the skies are clear, and pointing the way on stormy nights even if only with glimpses.

This is essential for every organization. It is even more critical for the stability of a nation. Consider the United States as an example. The Constitution has served this role for America since 1789. For 229 years when our nation has faced a question, the best and brightest minds of that era have asked: What does the Constitution say about this? How does the Constitution guide us in this matter? A thousand years from now, unimaginable civilizations will marvel at the genius of the United States Constitution.

Mission is the foundation of a Dynamic Culture. One clear mission is essential to the success of any organization. The supremacy of mission should never be questioned. The greatest organizations, with the most Dynamic Cultures, don't talk about work; they talk about mission. There are few things more powerful than a common unchanging purpose—a mission. Men and women on a mission behave very differently than men and women who are simply going to work.

Whatever your organization does, there is a way to focus on mission. Getting clear about it, crowning mission king, and making the connection between your organization's mission and the work every single team member does every day is essential to building a Dynamic Culture in which people love coming to work and accomplishing great things together. Organize everyone's work for maximum mission impact, and the more people realize they are adding value, the better they will feel about themselves, their roles, and the organization.

How many T-shirt organizations do you think there are in the world? Right, too many to count. Then there is the Life is Good organization. What do they do? On one level they just make T-shirts, like all the other T-shirt organizations. But how do they talk about what they do? They say things like "Spreading the power of optimism" and "Life is not perfect, life is not easy, but life is good."

Consider this paragraph from their website:

> We see it when we believe it. Each one of us has a choice: to focus our energy on obstacles or opportunities. To fixate on our problems, or focus on solutions. We can harp on what's wrong with the world (see most news media), or we can cultivate what's right with the world. What we focus on grows.

Let me remind you, *this is a T-shirt company!*

> That's why the Life is Good community shares one simple, unifying mission: to spread the power of optimism. Optimism is not irrational cheerfulness or "blind" positivity. It's a pragmatic strategy for approaching life.

How different do you think it is working for Life is Good compared to other T-shirt companies? Let's take it a step further and make it personal. How different do you think working for Life is Good is than working for your organization?

When I speak to people about making mission king and transforming their work into mission, they often roll their eyes or object that there is nothing inspiring about what they do. I listen respectfully and then disagree. No doubt some work is more inspiring and easier to consider a mission than other work. This is where inspiring nonprofits have a decided advantage. But all honest work can and should be mission focused.

Take the garbage collector, the example of examples. It's a role that has been immersed in a negative stigma since before you were born. How would your city look if no one picked up trash for a couple of weeks? One city got to find out: New York. Twice, actually. Get online and look at pictures of the 1968 and 1981 garbage strikes—be sure not to miss the pictures of what happened during the 1981 strike when a freak windstorm hit New York when there was a week's worth of trash on the ground.

Consider again for a moment how we've defined culture:

Culture is the vision, values systems, language, expectations, behaviors, and beliefs that increase or decrease an organization's chances of accomplishing its strategy and fulfilling its mission, which in turn increases or decreases how much people enjoy coming to work.

Culture makes organizations more effective or less effective, and it makes real people's lives more enjoyable or more miserable; there is no middle ground. It's easy to overlook the misery each decision we make at every level of an organization can cause real people and real families.

Dynamic Cultures and mission-focused organizations go hand in hand. They value mission impact above all else. They make mission king—and they protect their king, always. But the main reason they do this is because it ensures sustainability. Making mission king is like the farmer who stores grain for the winter, grain to use as seed in the spring, and grain for the following winter just in case he has a poor crop next year. This farmer's family is never likely to go hungry. They may go without some of the niceties of life, but they will not go without the necessities. Like all good things, sustainability—the long view—requires sacrifice. The long view always does.

Dynamic Cultures make sustainability a priority by making mission king, greatly reducing the chances that workers and families will experience misery, which wears a thousand different masks. That kind of misery is the result of making something or someone other than mission king.

Again, it is a mistake to think this is an issue just for leaders. Every person in an organization has a role to play in creating a Dynamic Culture. We have all encountered Culture Advocates and we have all encountered culture vampires, at every level within organizations.

As an employee, it is a mistake to think that your boss is king or queen. Always be respectful, but do not be afraid to propose an idea that will benefit the mission and improve the chances of success and sustainability. Don't just defer because she is your boss. Don't be a constant annoyance either, and certainly don't embarrass your leader in front of others. Know when to raise ideas. There is a time and a place. In most cases it is unwise and rude to contradict your boss in front of others. There are some cases in which you must do so if you know or see something essential and timely that he does not. Here I am thinking about our military clients. This may be a life-or-death situation, and everything changes then. But in business it is usually much wiser and more respectful to step aside with your leader after the meeting and make your point privately. I suspect you would like the same courtesy if you ever needed to be corrected.

Some leaders may find people who agree with everything they say convenient or expedient, but it is not good for the mission or the culture.

You don't want to work for a leader who wants to be surrounded by people who agree with everything he or she pronounces. These leaders despise people who slow them down with any kind of change to their own plan, regardless of how good the suggestion may be. Furthermore, they don't actually respect the people who act exactly the way they want them to act, agreeing with them and letting them do whatever they want. Business leaders like this consider themselves to be kings, and they are always willing to sacrifice their pawns for their own selfish advantage or simply to survive.

If you hold any type of leadership position yourself, remind people over and over again that you are not king. This gives them permission to do their best work and empowers them to do what is best for the mission in every situation—even if that means disagreeing with you. But beware: People will want to make you king (or queen). They will do it because too many organizations work this way. They will do it because they want to ingratiate themselves with you and curry favor, hoping you will help them sometime in the future to further their career. They will do it because it is a subtle and often subconscious way to reject accountability and place all the responsibility on your shoulders. As a leader, you should expect to be respected, but resist any and all attempts by anyone to make you king. Mission Is King.

"Matthew is not king!" I remind people of this a lot. You cannot say it too much. People have been pandering to foolish kings who have been abusing their power for thousands of years; it is deeply ingrained in the human gene pool. You need to remind them, over and over again, that Mission Is King.

There are lots of ways to say it. "When you make me king you hurt the mission." "If you make me king you hurt the organization, and then you make less money next year than you could have." People hear that last one loud and clear. The most effective way to serve your self-interest is to serve the mission.

Whatever you want for yourself—a pay raise, a promotion, or a certain opportunity—powerfully serving the mission is the best way to get it.

People will want to make you king because you are a leader. You have to proactively refuse. Letting them make you king is bad for you, it's bad for them, and it's bad for business. This concept is a touchstone that we will return to many times in our discussion of culture. It has far-reaching effects throughout any organization.

I can see when people are leaning in the direction of making me king, and I have to remind them again: "Matthew is not king!" It may become monotonous, but it needs to be vocalized, and once is not enough. You cannot just vaguely refer to it once and move on. Sometimes in meetings I will see the conversation veering down the wrong path, or notice that someone is hesitant to speak up. So I will ask the person, "Who is king around here?" She will reply that Mission Is King. "Good," I'll say. "So what are you thinking that you are not saying?" There is enough humor and enough seriousness in this exchange to liberate the person to say exactly what she is thinking.

Mission Is King, and culture is about mission.

The role of culture is to support the mission of an organization, to improve and increase the possibility of mission accomplishment . . . to make mission more effective and most successful. This in turn leads to more fulfilled and happier employees, better conversations at the dinner table, stronger families, better communities, and an economic-dominant nation.

Culture is *not* just a collection of personal preferences. This is one of the first points I made in our discussion of culture, because it is a trap so many organizations fall into. It's not about convenience, comfort, personal interest, or individual preferences. It's not about you and it's not about me. Culture is about mission.

The essential question when it comes to doing anything in relation to the culture is, "How will this help us better fulfill our mission?"

If you can convince me that bringing your dog to work will increase our chances of accomplishing our mission, then you have my attention. If wearing jeans makes it possible for you to better execute your work and increases the chances of mission success, then I am all for it. As a leader, I am not responsible for giving you everything you want like you're a tantrum-throwing five-year-old; I am responsible for making sure you have what you need to succeed (within the confines of the organization's limited resources). You may need a computer that doesn't crash every five minutes, or you may need more access to the leadership team. Different people need different things to succeed. It is a leader's role to have her finger on the pulse of those needs. And if you are a leader, don't assume people know what they need to succeed. Sometimes they don't. You will see things that they don't see because they are simply too close to it, or because they don't have the experience you have.

In a Dynamic Culture, people get hired and fired not because of whom they know, but because a leader believes they will add value that will increase the organization's chances of mission success. People get fired when it is determined that their presence is not sufficiently helping the team execute the mission, that their presence has become an active obstacle to the mission, or that they are poisoning the culture in some way.

The full implications of this single concept—Mission Is King—are so far-reaching that it is impossible to overestimate them. They are unending, in fact. The idea reaches further and further into the organization the more you reflect upon it and the more you implement it.

Think about office space for a minute. Have you ever tried to move someone from a private office to a cubicle? Not fun! The problem is that once upon a time we told them, "This is your office." That's where we made the mistake. All space is mission space. When you assign an office, you have to be clear about that. You have to verbalize it: "We are assigning this mission space for you to use at this time because we think it is the best use of this mission space at this time. There may be a time in the future when we discover that this office can better serve the mission in some other way."

Company cars and trucks, copy machines, phones, retail locations, billable hours, and everything down to the stapler— these are all mission resources. Take them out of the context of the mission your organization is trying to accomplish and your culture gets selfish and dysfunctional pretty quickly. Every resource should be deployed for the best mission outcome.

Everything belongs to the mission. Everyone and everything bows down to the mission. Everyone and everything serves the mission. Mission Is King. This is one of the most practical and powerful ideas you can apply in your organization. This is a game changer—for the organization as well as for the employees and leaders. So if you're not on board with the mission, it's probably a good idea to get off the bus.

Once mission is firmly established at the center of a culture, most things get a lot easier. It becomes easier to make decisions and easier to accept them. Mission-centric cultures also tend to have less conflict, less politics, less water-cooler gossip, and a healthier way of dialoguing when people do disagree about things that actually matter.

Margaret Mead, an American cultural anthropologist, wrote, "Never doubt that a small group of thoughtful, committed citizens can change the world. Indeed, it is the only thing that ever has." The important thing to understand is that every one of these world-changing groups had a very clear sense of mission. Making mission king is the way to accomplish incredible things with any group of people, small or large.

A dozen things will try to distract you from your mission every day. It is amazing how difficult it is to keep the main thing the main thing. Stay focused on your mission.

A Dynamic Culture's Three Best Friends

One of the most difficult decisions very talented people have to make during their careers is whether to practice, teach, or research. There is no wrong decision, but every industry and every society needs people to dedicate their lives to each of these.

Every person in our society today either has had a personal encounter with cancer or knows someone who has cancer. The result is that our age yearns for a cure. In order to cure cancer, we need some of the most talented doctors to stop seeing patients so they can go into laboratories and study endlessly what their peers are discovering, gradually discovering for themselves new things about cancer (sometimes tiny things), which the next researcher puts together with another tiny thing he or she has been working on, and so on, with each discovery putting us one step closer to a cure. Along the way, particular forms of cancer become much more treatable and manageable. There are types of cancer that would have killed you fifty years ago that are completely treatable today, because of this type of shared, progressive research.

The thing is, those research doctors had to stop seeing patients. You cannot see patients all day if you are going to do that type of research. A doctor who sees patients all day long focuses on the effects of cancer. It is good, noble, and necessary work. The doctor who steps away from attending to her patients every day and walks into the solitude of a research lab—which is also good, noble, and necessary work—to focus on what causes cancer is the long-term play.

The principle of causation, or cause and effect, is one of the governing principles of the universe. If I drop a raw egg on cement, it will break. The cause: I dropped the egg. The effect: It splattered everywhere.

World-class cultures are interested in causes. They understand if you deal with the cause, the effect will also be dealt with appropriately. However, many leaders and HR professionals constantly race around dealing with the effects of dysfunctional and unhealthy cultures, rather than pausing long enough to consider the actual causes of these effects. The six principles that make up the culture solution are aimed at changing that.

There are some telltale signs of world-class cultures. One of the easiest ways to identify a culture pursuing excellence is simply the number of people who bring pen and paper to a meeting, speech, or conference and actively take notes. I can typically predict the trajectory of a person's career with this one question: Do you actively or passively participate in meetings and events? Many make the mistake of thinking active participation means saying something, but that is not so. Taking notes is active participation. Listening—really listening—and considering what is being said and how it can improve what you and your team are doing is active participation. When I stand up to speak to a room full of people and everyone has arms folded in the mental posture of, "Who is this guy and what has he got for me?" I know there is a high likelihood that I am in a culture of mediocrity.

Every week there are new articles that list the qualities of great cultures. These lists include things like: people are happy; high engagement; low turnover; minimal politics; many people applying for roles; people see their work as more than just a job; high trust and transparency, leading to minimization of fear; employees feel appreciated; people have fun at work. There is nothing wrong with these things, but too many people read these articles and think they need to find new ways to "have more fun at work." The problem is that these things are not usually mission-centric; in fact, often they are not related to any organizational priority at all. They are based on the false assumption that the articles are based on: Inject these things into your organization and you will have a world-class culture. In reality, the things listed are just the natural effects of a mission-centric, people-centric culture. They are the *effect*, not the *cause*.

There are just as many articles outlining the symptoms of sick, twisted, and toxic corporate cultures: your boss takes credit for your work and ideas; scapegoating; you feel sick when you think about going to work; anyone with any talent leaves; politics is rampant and tolerated (or even encouraged); lack of loyalty; gossip, backbiting, and passive-aggressive communication; people are miserable and afraid to share ideas. Again, there is nothing wrong with pointing these things out. But it is critical that we realize that these are the *symptoms*, not the *disease*; the *effects*, not the *cause*.

These articles are also usually accompanied by advice on how to survive toxic cultures. My advice is simple: Don't just survive.

Do something about it. Cancer is the number one cause of death around the globe; it is the number one cause of cultural death too. Do you know who or what is the cancer in your organization's culture? Whose role is it to identify that cancer and perform the surgery to remove it? Regardless of your place or position in the organization, become a Culture Advocate. Otherwise get the heck out of that place ASAP. Life is too short to be miserable at work.

This book is not about the effects of good and bad cultures. It is about the primary causes. It is concerned with what causes an organization's culture to become great and how everyone involved in the organization can start practicing and encouraging these essential causes today. In this quest, you and your culture have three best friends.

Best Friend No. 1: A Hunger for Best Practices

Only fools start from scratch. Legendary champions, explorers, scientists, and those who achieve monumental success in any field do it by standing on the shoulders of giants. A talented young basketball player who ignored everything that the greats who have gone before him had achieved would become above average at best. Someone who set out to climb Mount Everest without studying those who had succeeded and failed before would be a fool. A scientist who set out to cure cancer and wanted to start from scratch and ignore everything thousands of other scientists have already learned about cancer would be considered a joke.

People who are serious about succeeding at anything are hungry for best practices. They never start from scratch at anything. Someone hungry for best practices is constantly asking herself: What is the best way to do this? Who is the best in the world at this, and what can I learn from that person? They always have someone to learn from before they begin anything.

Ask someone who is hungry for best practices to ship a hundred thousand packages a day and he will immediately ask himself, "How do Amazon and UPS do that, and what can I learn from them?" Ask someone hungry for best practices who has never run a marathon to run a marathon and she will ask herself, "Who is the best in the world at training novices to run marathons?" Ask somebody hungry for best practices who has absolutely no experience with copywriting to write copy for a new brochure about the organization, and that person googles "best brochures ever written about organizations"; "how to write a great brochure for your product"; "world-class copywriting techniques"; "biggest mistakes first-time copywriters make."

The idea of studying best practices (whether for five minutes or five hours) before beginning anything is one that most people say they subscribe to, but it is not employed anywhere near enough.

Anytime someone brings me substandard work, I ask, "What was your process for arriving at this?" Often the answer is another question: "What do you mean?" This is usually an ominous start, but not always. Getting people to describe their "work process" teaches you more about a person than two years of regular business interaction with that person. It allows you to understand how they work and how they think about complex problems, but it also allows you to help them improve their work process. This is the ultimate cause and effect when it comes to the work an individual (or team) produces. Help someone improve their work process and you forever improve every piece of work they bring you.

As an author, I am fascinated with writing process. Every author has one; the best evolve over time. But in many cases, I am much more interested in reading about an author's writing process than I am in reading their books. Hemingway had some fabulous triggers that would break through writer's block, and he had the discipline to stop in the middle of a great idea so the next day he could start with momentum. Most writers write until the well is empty, and the next day when they sit down they start on empty and struggle to get into it. Many writers have a whole regimen around their daily writing process. Some authors have a unique way of planning a book, routines that surround how they treat a third draft versus a second draft, or rituals they employ when starting or finishing a book. The great Australian novelist Morris West used to sit with his finished typed manuscript on his desk and gently pat it like you would a puppy or even a child.

The point is writing a great book isn't just about sitting down and letting inspiration flow onto the page. Like any other work, it requires inspiration, yes, but mostly disciplined hard work. Writing a book is easily romanticized. That's why most people who start never finish. There are some great moments. When you first conceive the idea for a book, it is magical and very exciting. Finishing a book can be very satisfying, but it isn't always, because you never are quite able to get it down on the page the way it exists in your head. But mostly, writing a book is just really hard work.

Work process is everywhere, and it is fascinating. How did Picasso work? What was his process? Einstein? Galileo? Leonardo da Vinci? How does Bono write a song? What's his process? You can learn so much from a person's work process. Do you know your own? Have you consciously developed one? Good news: If you haven't, you haven't even come close to doing your best work yet.

If you are a leader, help the men and women you lead

develop a strong work process that works for them, and encourage them to organize their time and energy around that process for the best results.

Part of every successful person's work process is an examination of best practices. It is a great starting point for any project. Wherever you find excellence, you find a hunger for best practices; when this hunger is absent, you usually find mediocrity. Too many people want to do things their way rather than the best way. It is a leading indicator of arrogance and mediocrity. By ensuring Mission Is King and remains so, we automatically build humility into the culture. It doesn't matter how you prefer to do something. What matters is outcome. What way of doing things will produce the most mission impact?

Every day we encounter dozens of opportunities, both personally and professionally, to engage the principle of best practices. Leveraging this principle creates a tremendous advantage, increases our chances of success, drives excellence, saves time, and improves results. Activating a curiosity about best practices should be the first task for every one of our projects. Who is the best in the world at this and what can I learn from her? Drive this behavior deep into your work process and deep into the work process of every member of your team and organization. It's time to stop talking about best practices and actually leverage this powerful principle in everything we do.

Best Friend No. 2:
Commitment to Continuous Learning

The less people read, the more boring they tend to become, and the less continuous learning is celebrated in an organization, the more boring it tends to become. And I don't recommend boring your customers. They are unlikely to hang around for too long if you do. If you are a nonprofit, if your donors find your organization boring, you're going to be in trouble before too long.

It is a myth that a really successful continuous learning program costs a lot of money. Should you pay my colleagues and me to come in from time to time and do some great training and coaching? Yes. But the easiest way to foster this behavior on an ongoing basis is with books. And books are cheap.

How many books does the average person on your team read each year? The answer is probably "not enough." Continuous learning is essential to a vibrant, healthy Dynamic Culture. And the easiest and cheapest way to encourage that is with books. For twenty dollars, you have the world's leading expert on almost any topic teaching you.

People often ask me why I speak more about continuous learning than I do about continuous improvement. Well, if you cast your mind back to our discussion about causality, or the cause-and-effect relationship that exists in everything, you will find your answer. It is continuous learning (the cause) that leads to continuous improvement (the effect).

People's lives are busier than ever before, both personally and professionally. This is the main obstacle to continuous learning. As you establish priorities in your life and help your team and colleagues to do the same, this will help. But let's be honest, our lives are not going to become simpler and less hectic overnight simply by setting priorities and boundaries. So, there is a central principle that applies here and to so many other things when it comes to the success of an organization (person or team) and building a Dynamic Culture: Don't let what you can't do interfere with what you can do. You may not have the time or the resources to get an MBA, but you can make the time and you do have the resources to read five pages of a great book every day.

Do you feel overwhelmed? Are you thinking, "I can't do that"? Throughout this book, you should be thinking over and over again, "I can do that." Building a Dynamic Culture should be approached little by little and should not be overwhelming. At no point throughout this book should you feel overwhelmed or think, "That's impossible; we could never do that; this is completely overwhelming." If you start to feel that way, you have missed the message. Over and over again as you make your way through this book, I hope you will be thinking to yourself, "I can do that."

Our lives change when our habits change. This one habit—reading five pages a day—will have a huge impact on your life and your organization. If you can cultivate this habit, you will be amazed how your knowledge and enthusiasm for life and your professional career will increase. Just five pages a day. I hope you're thinking, "I can do that." Five pages a day for a year is 1,825 pages a year, 18,250 pages in a decade, and 45,625 pages over twenty-five years. That's 228 books with an average length of 200 pages.

If you asked most people to read 45,625 pages of material, they would be completely overwhelmed. If you asked most people to commit to reading 228 books, they would feel utterly intimidated. But five pages a day, we can do that. Continuous learning makes incredible things possible.

How would your life be different one year from now, five years from now, ten years from now if you read five pages of a great book each day? How would your organization be different if everyone adopted just this one habit? They don't all need to be business books; in fact, they shouldn't be. Reading a broad range of books encourages innovation and creativity. More and more people don't read at all, and too many others have reduced their whole reading experience to six-hundred-word articles that at best give a cursory look at a subject, and at worst encourage the type of shallow and superficial approach that you want to cast far away from your culture. Books provide a depth that is needed to drive real, continuous learning and improvement. Books change our lives, because we become the books we read.

Continuous learning is a leading indicator of organizational health, so it is essential to know that it is one of your best friends as you set out to build a Dynamic Culture—and the easiest way to foster that is to get your people reading books.

Best Friend No. 3: Treat People like People

The truth is, I'm embarrassed that I even need to mention the importance of treating people like people, but when it comes to building a Dynamic Culture, this is your very best friend. Let's face it, people don't exist for organizations; organizations exist for people. People don't exist for work; work exists for people. The larger an organization becomes, the easier it is for that organization to become soulless and without conscience. So I will not pretend it is not easier to create a Dynamic Culture in a small organization.

If you are part of a huge organization, focus your Culture Advocate efforts where you have the most influence. Start with your team or department. Create a subculture that intrigues and fascinates everyone else in the organization. Extraordinary effectiveness is usually the result of focusing our efforts where we have the most influence. If you have the most influence with three or four people, start there. Don't let what you can't do interfere with what you can do. You cannot change a culture overnight, even if you own it or are its CEO. But we can all be Culture Advocates to varying extents by focusing our culture-changing efforts where we have the most influence.

You may say, "I have no influence over anyone." That is not true, but let's assume it is for a moment. You have total influence over yourself; start there. Create a one-man or one-woman culture that is exactly how you would like the whole organization's culture to be.

Once upon a time there was a very successful business owner. His organization had faithfully served millions of customers for many, many years. But lately, business had not been so good, and his competitors were just waiting for him to fail. For weeks and months, the man pondered the crisis, but the problems were so complex, and solutions seemed nowhere to be found.

Everyone was wondering what would happen to this great organization, so finally the businessman announced that he was hosting a dinner for all his employees, where he would unveil a plan to save the organization and return it to its former glory. He wanted to convey to them how important each person was to the future success of the organization.

The morning of the dinner, he was sitting in his study at home working on his speech, when his wife came in and asked if he would mind watching their son for a few hours while she ran some errands. He was about to say, "I really need to focus on finishing my speech," but something caught his tongue and he found himself agreeing, reluctantly.

His wife had only been gone about ten minutes when there was a knock on the study door, and there appeared his seven-year-old son. "Dad, I'm bored!" he exclaimed. The father spent the next couple of hours trying to amuse his son while also trying to finish his speech. Finally, he realized that if he could not find some way to entertain his child, he was never going to get his speech finished in time.

Picking up a magazine, he thumbed through the pages until he came to a large, brightly colored map of the world. He ripped the picture into dozens of pieces, and led his son into the living room. Then, throwing the pieces all over the floor, he announced, "Son, if you can put the map of the world back together I will give you twenty dollars."

The boy immediately began gathering the pieces. He was keen to earn the extra money, as he needed just twenty more dollars to buy a toy he had been saving for since his last birthday. The father returned to his study, thinking he had just bought himself a couple of hours to finish working on his speech, because he knew his seven-year-old son had no idea what the map of the world looked like.

But five minutes later, just as he was settling into his speech, there was another knock on the study door. There stood the young boy, holding the completed map of the world.

The father said in amazement, "How did you finish it so quickly?" The boy smiled and said, "You know, Dad, I had no idea what the map of the world looked like, but as I was picking up the pieces, I noticed that on the back there was a picture of a man." The father smiled, and the boy continued. "So, I put a sheet of paper down, and I put the picture of the man together, because I knew what the man looked like. I put another sheet of paper on top, then holding them tightly I turned them both over."

He smiled again and exclaimed, "I figured, if I got the man right, the world would be right!"

The man handed his son twenty dollars. "And you've given me my speech for tonight: If you get the man right, you get the world right."

When we focus our efforts on influencing who and what we can most influence—ourselves—we tend to have the most impact. You are the epicenter of your universe of influence.

I don't like speaking in absolutes. In my twenties, I was so sure of so many things. Now in my mid-forties, it seems I am sure of less and less each year. But I am certain of this: You cannot and will not build a Dynamic Culture if you don't treat people like people.

Phenomenal business cultures engage the soul of every employee and customer, so much so that *the customers feel like they are part of the organization*. Every organization wants its employees to treat its customers and clients with great humanity. But you simply cannot expect that to happen consistently unless you first treat your people like people. Most employees treat customers the same way they are treated by their leader (or organization).

When we treat people like people, they behave like people. When we forget this crucial concept, we forget that life is messy and everyone has something going on. Whatever that something is, it's their biggest challenge or heartache right now. That includes your leader and even your CEO. No title can shield you from the brutality of life at times. Every person in your organization is carrying a heavy burden, and in most cases, you are not even aware of it. They don't talk about it, but that doesn't mean they don't spend most of their days with it in the back of their minds. Most people's lives are quite difficult. The moment an organization stops treating people like people, the moment an organization forgets that life is difficult and everyone is carrying a heavy load, that is the moment when the soul of an organization dies—and anything that is soulless is dead, or soon will be.

When my book *The Dream Manager* was first released, I was surprised by how well it was received. One thing in particular caught my attention. The essence of the message the book conveys is: *If you treat people like people by helping them identify their dreams and encouraging them to chase those dreams, employee engagement will go through the roof.* This just seemed obvious to me, so I have to confess I was surprised—no, stunned—at how many people saw this approach as brilliant and revolutionary.

The reaction to that book and the response to the concept itself screamed at me: In the context of being successful and profitable, we have long forgotten how to treat people like people. For six hundred years we have been trying to separate the personal from the professional, but as I explained in *Off Balance*, this is a fool's errand. The latest and most comprehensive example of this fiasco has been the whole work-life balance conversation and obsession.

Our work is a big, important part of our life. You simply cannot separate the personal and professional aspects of a person's life. If an employee has a child sick at home, she will disengage from her work. If an employee has a parent who is dying, he will be disengaged (to some extent) from his work. It is natural, normal, rational, human, and actually the smart thing to do. It is a survival mechanism. And it doesn't matter if the employees just described are the CEO or line workers in the factory.

By the same token, when things are going really well at work, a person is more likely to have a thriving marriage and dynamic relationships with his children, and to be more engaged in his health and well-being, to name but a few of the benefits of enjoyment and engagement at work.

Flip the coin one more time and you discover that when a team member is thriving in her personal life, she will bring that great energy to work and be more engaged than ever. What happens to people personally impacts their professional engagement, and vice versa.

Treating people like people is good for business, not to mention that it is just the right thing to do. And I don't know about you, but I'd like to be part of more organizations that do things for that reason alone: It is just the right thing to do.

But let me issue a warning: If we continue to ignore this central lesson and treat people not like people, but like *mere* employees, instruments, or, at worst, objects, they will increasingly stop behaving like people. Sooner or later they will start behaving like animals. We have all encountered organizations where the employees behave like feral cats— and I choose that simile very specifically and with great intentionality. Feral cats are usually domestic cats that have been abandoned. Loved and cared for once, they are now forgotten and neglected, left to fend for themselves. When people approach feral cats, the cats will either hiss or run away and hide. If they are cornered or trapped, they cower and tremble out of uncontrolled fright. Their offspring (new hires) very quickly adopt all the same behavioral traits.

This is obviously an extreme example of what happens in the unhealthiest cultures. But if you hire a new team member who has come from a feral environment, you need to be mindful of that. This person will not respond as you would expect—even to good things—until he has recovered from the feral experience and gained trust in the new culture.

It is so easy to forget the complexities of each and every person's life. Last week I was flying into a city one night and looking down at all those homes and wondering what was going on inside each of them. Is a family having dinner together? Is a couple fighting about getting divorced? Are others trying to put their relationship back together? There's a teenage girl down there scared out of her mind to tell her parents she is pregnant. There are other women desperate to have babies who are struggling with infertility. Some children are being loved and cherished; others are being ignored, neglected, or worse. Some people are probably working and enjoying it; others are working and resenting it. Some are reading; more are watching television. Some are making love. There are people struggling with depression, alcoholism, and various medical problems. Someone down there is in his final wrestle with death, perhaps grateful and peaceful or possibly filled with regret. Others are gripped with worry about how they are going to pay the bills this month . . . and it goes on and on.

Life is messy, and complicated. Most of those people will get up and go to work tomorrow. Some love their work; others hate it. Some have a fabulous relationship with their leader, and others can't stand the person they report to. Forty percent of them are looking for another role.

This is the bottom line.

1. People don't come to work for your organization because they love working for your organization. They might—if they do, I am happy for them and happy for you—but that

is not the primary reason people come to work for your organization.

2. People don't come to work for your organization because they love their work. They might—if they do, I am happy for them—but that is not the primary reason people come to work for your organization.

3. And as hard as it might be for some leaders to accept, people don't come to work for your organization because they love working with their leaders. They might—if they do, I am happy for them—but that is not the primary reason people come to work for your organization.

So, why do people come to work? It would be easy to say to make money, but it is so much more than that. The primary reason people come to work is because they have dreams for themselves and dreams for their families, and they believe that by hitching their wagon to your organization those dreams will be advanced or realized.

In most cases people's dreams are simple and achievable. They want to own a home, pay off credit card debt or student loans, or take their kids on an amazing vacation or any vacation. They want to buy their spouse an unexpected gift, send their children to a better school, or save enough money to enjoy retirement. There are an infinite number of variations, but they are deeply personal to the individual. People's dreams are what get them up in the morning for work; it's these dreams that get them to show up for work even when their leader treats them poorly. It's these dreams that they think about when their work seems tedious or intolerable. It's all about dreams.

How do I know all this is true? Well, consider your own situation, whether you are the CEO or the janitor. What are your dreams? If working for your organization stopped helping you to accomplish those dreams, what would you do? If the organization were outrageously lucky, you would just leave quickly and quietly. But more likely, you would slowly disengage, poison the well by telling anyone who would listen about your dissatisfaction, which would increase their dissatisfaction, and finally leave when either it became too painful to handle anymore or another opportunity presented itself.

Hunger for best practices and commitment to continuous learning are both very good friends when it comes to building a Dynamic Culture, but your best friend is treating people like people. It's a simple concept, but don't confuse simple with easy. Making people feel that their unique contribution matters, and doing it with integrity, is the master touch of all great coaches, mentors, and leaders.

What matters most? People. Life and business teaches us that quickly if we are coachable. After that, what matters most in the life of an organization? Mission. Gather together a group of people, large or small, define the mission clearly, relentlessly pursue that mission, and you will witness amazing things. Wherever you work, whatever you do, it's time to get really clear about what the mission is, make mission king, and protect your king. This is the focus and discipline that leads to Dynamic Cultures where people love coming to work to accomplish great things together.

The Second Principle:
MISSION IS KING

4

what's the plan?

Of Course Strategy Matters

When Peter Drucker said, "Culture eats strategy for breakfast," the comment wasn't intended to undermine the importance of strategy. Strategy is incredibly important. You cannot overestimate its importance, and that's what makes the quote so powerful.

The very idea that something else was anywhere near as important as strategy initially stunned people. The statement was arresting. When it was first heard it would have felt like a category 6 earthquake to any organizational management expert, or as if the earth had just shifted off its axis. It was a radical statement—and the thing about radical ideas is they don't lose their flavor over time. "Culture eats strategy for breakfast." It is more relevant today than ever before, given the growing dysfunction of employees' personal lives. Whether Drucker said it or not, if he were alive today, he would probably say, "Culture eats strategy for breakfast, lunch, and dinner."

It is essential to understand that the more dysfunctional people's personal lives become, the more critical healthy corporate cultures become. People do bring all the joy and misery of their personal lives to work. *A Dynamic Culture needs to be able to absorb the dysfunction of people's personal lives in a way that allows them to still perform their work at a high level.* This is an incredibly complex thought, and one that I usually would not even include. It's a topic someone should write a doctoral thesis on. It needs to be said, understood, and acted upon. Or we can continue to hide behind the nonsensical excuse that this is not a corporate responsibility. In nirvana that is true, but it's probably best if we stay as closely connected to reality as possible.

Warning: If you are not in a leadership position, you may be tempted to check out now, thinking the topic of strategy doesn't matter to your role. Please don't make that mistake.

In the opening of the book I wrote: *Too many books are written just for leaders; as a result, the message never makes it all the way through the organization. That's why I specifically set out to write this book for everyone in your organization.*

If you are not in a leadership role, there are a dozen reasons you should keep reading, but let me just give you the single most compelling reason. You may not have a leadership role in the business you work for, but the most important business of your life is the business of your life itself. Anything you learn about corporate strategy should teach you to live your own life more strategically. Great businesses have Strategic Plans, and they update them at least once a year.

The biggest project or venture you are running is your life. Do you have a plan? Most people don't. They are just stumbling from one year to the next, hoping for the best. That is merely an observation, not a judgment. More than most, I have seen how brutal ordinary life can be, even in the suburbs of American cities. At the same time, I want to encourage you to start developing a Personal Strategic Plan (PSP).

Toward the end of each year I get together with a small group to start working on my PSP for the coming year, but also to look back at the previous year's PSP and see how we did. On the first day of January we share our PSPs and hold one another accountable. I also give my coach a copy of my PSP so he can know exactly what I am out to accomplish in the coming year.

The point is simple. Strategy and planning are important for organizations, *and even more important for our lives*. And yet, most people spend more time planning their annual vacation than they spend planning their lives.

"Culture eats strategy for breakfast." The maxim does not mean strategy doesn't matter. There is no point having an exceptional culture and no strategy. And your organization will not withstand bad strategic decisions, regardless of how strong and healthy your culture is. But when you have a solid strategy, developing a Dynamic Culture is like adding steroids.

Is culture more important than strategy? There is obviously no point having the best culture in the world if you have a horrible strategy, and vice versa. Our goal should be to build a world-class culture to execute a best-in-industry strategy.

But tragically, rigorous planning is neglected by far too many organizations of all sizes. And intentional culture development is neglected by even more. And even those that do take the time to develop worthy Strategic Plans often mismanage or ignore those plans once the exercise is complete.

So, let us follow the advice of the king from *Alice in*

Wonderland: "Begin at the beginning . . . and go on till you come to the end: then stop."

To begin, this first question may be somewhat awkward, but in my work as a consultant I have learned not to assume anything. Do you have a plan? This may seem like an infantile question, especially to smart people with lower rank in an organization. I ask the question because I am astounded by the number of organizations that don't have a Strategic Plan, and of those that do, I am further astounded that the plan is significantly out of date or that it takes so long to locate a copy of it when I request one.

Recently, I was working with a new client whose sales team FLOYD is coaching. Just in casual conversation I had mentioned, "It might be helpful if I could take a look at your Strategic Plan and make sure what we are doing aligns with what your leadership and board envision for the next one to three years." This $300 million organization had no Strategic Plan. I had to try not to look surprised; I'm pretty sure I failed.

Now, you don't need to feel embarrassed if you don't have a Strategic Plan. But I would suggest you do something about it, for reasons that I think will become self-evident in the coming pages. You don't need to go out and hire a big-six consulting organization and spend a fortune developing a Strategic Plan. But you do need to invest in this, and that investment will take two forms.

First, if you are a business owner, leader, or aspiring leader, you need to invest some time thinking about it. Read at least ten articles discussing strategic planning online, all of which will contradict each other, but all of which will have a couple of points worth thinking about.

Next, eventually you do need to spend some money on it. The first time around, you will be fine on your own, but when you come to the end of the year, you will discover you got distracted by business cycles, unexpected opportunities, or some type of crisis. So, if you don't want to spend the money the first time around, you should the second time. The plan will be better with an external participant guiding you through the process, probing your assumptions, and questioning your capacity. We help many organizations develop Strategic Plans; it is incredibly fulfilling work and amazing to see how the right Strategic Plan can impact an organization.

Now, if you work for a large corporation, you may have considered the preceding discussion to be remedial, but I would encourage you not to be so quick to judge. Your Fortune 500 company may have spent six or even seven figures with one of the most expensive consulting organizations in the world to develop an astounding Strategic Plan—but when was the last time you saw someone carrying a copy of it into a meeting? When was the last time it was referred to not in a cursory way, but specifically? Have you ever actually seen it? Have you even seen the part that pertains to your department or project?

Here's the thing—it doesn't matter if you are running a smallish family business or working for one of the biggest organizations in the world; regardless of size, a plan is essential to the success of a business. The planning process helps leaders to get very clear about what matters most and what matters least now. It helps them to envision where the organization is going over the next one to three years, outlines to some extent how they will get there, and provides a Scorecard.

So, the first point is: A great Strategic Plan can make all the difference. If you don't have one, get one. If you have one, start using it. We will talk more about how to do that most effectively in the coming chapters.

The second point is: Where is culture in the plan? Most organizations leave it out. They focus on sales and marketing, manufacturing and sourcing, financial reports and new product development, and other such things. But if you raise your hand when the plan is finished and say, "We say that culture is important and that we are committed to building a strong and healthy culture, but where is culture in our Strategic Plan?" you are likely to be greeted by a very, very awkward silence.

I have seen organizations who have culture plans that are separate from their Strategic Plan. The reason is usually because a culture plan tends to last a lot longer than a Strategic Plan. Who we are doesn't change that much; what we do might. I have seen other organizations that include their culture plan in their Strategic Plan. And I have seen both be successful.

Culture deserves a place in everything your organization does. Your organization deserves it. And not just any place—a primary place, a driving place. Everything your organization does affects culture, and culture affects everything your organization does. Culture should have a seat of honor at every planning meeting. Tape a sign that reads CULTURE to an empty chair and put that chair in a place of honor at meetings. When it comes to culture, we either need to get serious or shut up and stop talking about it. But be warned, there are dire consequences to the latter, and we have already seen how empty culture talk impacts employee and customer engagement.

A good Strategic Plan brings confidence to the culture. Confidence—now, that is something people can smell on their leaders. No amount of perfume or cologne can overshadow that smell. It is impossible to overestimate what that confidence means to an organization. Have you ever been around an elite athlete who has lost his or her confidence after an injury? It's not pretty.

Everyone around him is on eggshells in the gym, on the field, in the cafeteria, in the parking lot; his doubts, his insecurity, and his wondering whether he will ever make it back are palpable.

Great cultures are confident and humble at the same time. They are so confident, they don't need pretense, and so they very naturally embrace humility. A great product, service, leader, and strategy can all contribute to building confidence in an organization, but it is the culture that sustains organizational confidence.

Does strategy matter? Of course it does. It matters a great deal. But whatever your product or service is, whatever your strategy is, whatever your goals and mission are, nothing is more essential in accomplishing them than a strong, healthy, vibrant Dynamic Culture. We have to stop seeing culture as something that is at odds with strategy. They should be best friends. By forming strong connections between strategy and culture, and making mission king, you give everyone a clear sense of the what, the how, and the why.

The quintessential question is: Will culture be part of our strategy, or will strategy be part of our culture? The answer is both. It is not a one-way street.

Mission Is King, and both strategy and culture serve it. Strategy is the short-term way an organization accomplishes its mission. Culture should be included in every Strategic Plan. If you separate culture from strategy, you run the risk of culture going rogue and usurping the mission of the organization.

Who you are is infinitely more important than what you do. This is true for people and organizations. Wise organizations allow who they are to determine what they do. Strong, healthy, dynamic, enduring organizations adopt strategies that are a natural extension of their mission and culture. Strategy is what they do; mission and culture is who they are.

This powerful alignment of culture and strategy will create a competitive advantage of monumental proportions. An organization that takes this single idea seriously dominates its competition in attracting talent. An organization where Mission Is King and culture is central is so much stronger, healthier, more vibrant, and more dynamic than its competition. This type of organization deals with challenges and conflict in a very different way than its competition. And perhaps most convincingly, in a world where the speed of change has become immeasurable, an organization that makes mission king and forms this powerful alliance between culture and strategy deals with change infinitely more effectively than its competition. The most obvious example of this is that everyone is not waiting around for the king to make decisions about everything. As a culture matures in healthy and effective ways, more people are empowered to make more and more decisions.

For too long, in too many organizations of every type, culture has been considered the weak, unprofitable, distracting little brother to strategy. Not so. Real strength, enduring profitability, extraordinary employee engagement, and the next great idea that carries your organization into the future are much more likely to flow from a Dynamic Culture. The little brother has grown up and it turns out he is a genius. His name is Dynamic Culture.

Every organization needs a Strategic Plan. Napoleon reportedly said, "Those who fail to plan can plan to fail." He was right, but he failed anyway. Great plans spring forth from Dynamic Cultures. Napoleon had the wrong vision and values. He was culturally bankrupt. He wouldn't have been able to run a fast-food restaurant, let alone a nation. We are talking about a man who reinstituted slavery just eight years after it had been abolished; divorced his wife because she didn't give birth to a son; deprived women of their individual rights; rigged elections to continue his dictatorial regime; censored and then took control of the press; was self-congratulatory; sacrificed the lives of five hundred thousand men to invade Russia even after his advisers warned him that would be the cost; a man who said, "I care only for people who are useful to me—and only so long as they are useful."

Napoleon had a plan, but his strategy was self-serving and his culture was sick because his values were sick. These are just some of the reasons he failed. It is not enough just to have a plan. It is not enough just to have a strategy, even if it is a good one. Without a Dynamic Culture you are susceptible to failure. Sooner or later, a competitor will emerge who integrates mission, strategy, and culture, and that competitor will crush all others.

Every organization needs a Strategic Plan, and part of that plan should be the creation and growth of a Dynamic Culture. It doesn't matter how simple the first iteration of that plan might be. Twenty years ago, I sat in a food court in Washington, D.C., with a guy, and together we wrote the first Strategic Plan for an organization. It took me ten years to get that organization started, but today, just ten years later, it dominates its industry. Your first Strategic Plan can be simple, but let it be driven by who you are (values and culture) and not just what you do or how you do it (strategy).

Who Knows the Plan?

We can all agree that there is no point having a great Strategic Plan if nobody knows about it. Imagine having a bank account in your name that you have full access to—all you have to do is walk in and ask for the money—but you don't know about it.

Now, if that account has twenty-five dollars in it, it probably doesn't matter that much. But what if the bank account had ten million dollars in it? I suspect your attitude would change very quickly—mine would.

For most organizations, their Strategic Plan is like that second bank account. The only difference is that most good Strategic Plans are worth a lot more than ten million dollars, and the bigger the organization, the more zeros you can add to the end of that number.

Once an organization has gone through the process of developing a solid Strategic Plan, the next challenge is to communicate the plan to the organization. Some organizations—especially smaller ones—are able to share the whole plan with everyone. But depending on the size of the organization, that may not be helpful, necessary, or even possible (for legal, confidentiality, or proprietary reasons).

It is important, however, to realize that transparency is the new currency of trust in this society that has been let down (at best) and blatantly deceived (at worst) by almost every organization and profession with significant authority and responsibility. I won't say that trust in authority is at an all-time low in society, but it needs a revival, and that is especially true in the corporate world. So if the choice is between sharing more and sharing less, and the downside of sharing more is minimal, it is highly recommended that you take the path of sharing more.

The key is to cascade the Strategic Plan down through the organization, so that every leader, team, and employee is very clear about their role, authority, and accountability. Great organizations ensure every single person is clear about how he or she contributes to the success of the Strategic Plan.

Once everyone is clear about their role, solidify the connection between the Strategic Plan and the mission by talking about the plan as the most effective way at this moment to accomplish the mission. Do this whenever possible. The Strategic Plan is just a tool, and like everything and everyone else, it bows down to mission. The mission is always central and unchanging. Speak always first about mission, and then speak about the Strategic Plan in relation to it.

Whenever I speak about this topic, someone will inevitably stop me after my speech and say, "You didn't mention the customer." It's true. In this book and when I speak about this topic, I spend very little time talking about your customers. The reason is because I assume that your mission is to serve them powerfully, and that by getting clear about mission you either have or will get clear about how you can best serve your customers. But that is another book and another speech. Here we are focused on culture.

Communication is a huge piece of culture. So is trust. And communication fosters trust. Organizations that communicate well at all levels of the organization tend to be very trusted by employees. Dynamic Cultures have high trust levels. Culture Advocates do what they can to encourage this trust, and they avoid anything that erodes it.

Something as simple as gossip, which has become common in our society, is cancerous to an organization's culture. Gossip erodes trust. How do you know if it is gossip or just a discussion? If there is a problem and there is nobody in the conversation who can address the problem, it's gossip. If the person does not have a chance to defend his or her actions, it's gossip. It might seem like a little thing, but it isn't. You'd be amazed how much gossip goes on in the average organization, and how destructive it can be to people and the organization.

Create, communicate, and execute. These are the three essential phases of a Strategic Plan's life cycle. Yes, there may be changes, adjustments, refinements, and updates to deal with the unexpected, and other, finer points to the overall process. Any good plan is not static; it is a living, breathing document. But the way a Strategic Plan is created, communicated, adjusted, and executed determines whether it lives or dies, succeeds or fails.

Creating a good Strategic Plan can be exhausting; I have seen leadership teams collapse in a heap at the end of the process. I have also seen leadership teams excessively celebrate the completion of the creation of the plan. In that moment, I don't have the heart to tell them that the real work has not even begun yet. I let them enjoy their dinner and a few drinks, and save that message for the closing session the next day.

The most tragic thing I see happen with all too many Strategic Plans, some of them really good, is they get beautifully typeset and bound, and then thrown in some desk drawer, never to be mentioned or consulted again. And this happens often—in serious organizations.

The second tragedy that befalls Strategic Plans once they are completed is they get trapped in the upper regions of organizations, leaving the great majority of workers stumbling around in the dark trying to read their leaders' minds. It's important enough, so I'll say it again: There is no point in having a Strategic Plan if nobody knows about it.

If you want to know how well an organization is doing in this respect, there is a very simple test. Whether it is the organization you work for, one you volunteer for, or one you own, walk around and ask at least a dozen people, "What's the organization's most important goal this year?" You will be amazed by how many different answers you get. I am often saddened at how many people cannot even answer the question.

Once you have a viable Strategic Plan, you need the right communication campaign to cascade the message down through the organization. By all means, make it look like an important document, but then turn it into a living, breathing guidebook to a bigger, brighter future.

Creating a good Strategic Plan is a great start, but what matters most is what you do with it once you have it. Let's explore that together now.

The Not-So-Subtle Art of Overcommunication

We live in the age of communication, so it shouldn't be too difficult to communicate the plan to everyone in the organization, right? Wrong. When you were young, how many times did your mom have to ask you to do something before you did it? How many times do you have to ask your own children to do something before they start arguing about why they have to do it, never mind actually start doing it?

Those are fun questions. But now let's get serious. How many really good listeners do you know? I'm sad to say that although I have a lot of amazing people in my life, really good listeners are rare. Even most of my advisers and mentors—people I turn to for advice when an opportunity emerges or I am in a crunch to deal with a problem—are not great listeners. How many good listeners do you know?

Do you consider yourself a good listener? Do you check your email or text messages during meetings and conference calls? Do you ever find yourself thinking about something that happened yesterday or something you are looking forward to tonight instead of listening to someone who is speaking to you?

Most people think they are better at listening to others than they are. Research suggests that the average person listens with only 25 percent efficiency. That's a lot we are missing. If I'm an average listener, that means I miss 75 percent of what my colleagues or significant other tell me. It's astounding, really. Even worse, it means I probably miss 75 percent of what my children are trying to tell me.

If you have a child and you are an average listener, over the course of a lifetime you have missed three-quarters of what your son or daughter is trying to say to you. Even if you are twice as good at listening as the average listener, you've still missed half of what your child is trying to share with you. No wonder we have misunderstandings and disagreements.

If you want to be a better listener, I could tell you to be more empathetic, eliminate distractions so that you are present, remember you are not perfect, ask questions to gain further insight, not run from being uncomfortable, not change the subject, try not to be judgmental, not interrupt, and pause before responding. But what it all comes down to is getting *yourself* out of the way. It is not about you.

Why are most people such poor listeners? What is the key to becoming a great listener?

We get in the way. We think about ourselves rather than the person speaking. We get absorbed in how what is being said relates to us, rather than trying to work out how it relates to the person speaking. When we are preoccupied with ourselves, our thoughts, feelings, experiences, fears, ambitions, and everyday life all create noise and distractions that prevent us from *really* hearing what people are trying to tell us.

Listening is difficult. It's important to acknowledge that, because when we don't acknowledge that something is difficult, we don't allocate the necessary resources to succeed in that activity. To be a great listener requires patience, focus, awareness, and most of all it requires us to set aside our own agenda. It's natural that we see and experience life through the lens of self, and it's normal that we listen to what people are saying through that lens. But when we are able to set aside our own agenda and needs and focus on the other person, our listening skills increase exponentially. The best listeners set themselves aside.

To listen is an art and another essential life skill we fail to teach our young people. I am convinced that it is almost impossible to overstate the importance of listening as a life skill. Recently, a high school student asked me, "If you were me, what two skills would you work on improving?" I told him, "Decision-making and listening." These two skills intersect with every single aspect of life and business.

As we set out to communicate your Strategic Plan to the organization, it is *essential* to keep in mind the importance of listening, and to remember that people in general are not great listeners. You have something very important—your organization's Strategic Plan—that you need to communicate *very clearly* to your team or employees. The reality is that communicating a Strategic Plan in most organizations is like a huge game of Chinese Whispers. The point is—*it is incredibly difficult to convey a message to a group of people*. In fact, it usually requires a strategy of its own.

The solution is overcommunication.

One of my goals as a keynote speaker is for people to be able to remember a year later what I spoke about. Who was your keynote speaker at last year's event? Most people struggle to remember who the speaker was, let alone what he or she spoke about.

Repetition is your best friend when it comes to overcommunication. The truth is, most people are too proud to use this tool. But it works. We know this in our businesses. When it comes to branding and marketing, repetition is essential; failing to use it would guarantee failure. In fact, even in our marketing efforts most organizations change the message too often, because they lack the discipline to wait. We can't wait to change the message. It takes real discipline and humility to stick to one message and overcommunicate that message. A marketing message will seem stale to a marketing team long before that same message has reached deep into its target market, and an organizational message will seem stale to a leader long before it has reached deep into his or her team.

The concept of overcommunication is not about the quantity of information you share. It's about the number of times important information is conveyed.

If people don't know the plan, they can't execute it passionately.

The Third Principle:
OVERCOMMUNICATE THE PLAN

The best organizations with Dynamic Cultures have humility and discipline. Overcommunication takes humility because our minds tell us people will realize we already said that, and that they will think we don't know that we already said it. At first that may very well be the case, but over time people will realize that you are repeating yourself with great intentionality. It may not hurt to point out that you know you are repeating yourself, and you are doing it for a reason.

When it comes to overcommunication, you will have the greatest success if each time you share a message with an individual, your team, or the entire organization, you connect whatever you are trying to say to your organization's common, unchanging principle. This helps the listener put what you are saying in context, and leads to greater understanding, clarity, and stickiness.

It's fascinating that when it comes to branding and marketing we understand this principle without question. But when it comes to communicating with our own people (who very often are the consumers of our products), we throw this wisdom aside, abandoning the genius of simplicity for complexity.

Who is the best in the world at overcommunication? Coca-Cola.

There is a reason Coke is one of the most recognized and successful brands in the world. They will take a decade to drive a message deep into the culture. They'll take ten years to tell us something like, "It's the real thing." You have no idea how much humility, discipline, and intentionality it takes to do that. Coke's first slogan, in 1886, was "Drink Coca-Cola." It wasn't until eighteen years later, in 1904, that they changed it. What have they told us in the past fifty years? "Coke is it." "You can't beat the feeling." "Life tastes good." "Open happiness." "Taste the feeling."

Coca-Cola uses these slogans with the discipline of unerring repetition. The message is always simple—it has to be to get through all the cultural noise and lodge itself in the collective psyche. Simplicity and repetition are a brand's best friends.

They have been changing their slogan more often in the past

decade or so. Is that intentional and disciplined? Is it more effective? Or is their advertising agency like the stockbroker who doesn't understand that sometimes his or her job is to do nothing?

Most organizations change their slogans far too often. Just because your organization is very familiar with it does not mean your potential customers have heard the message yet. Great teachers use repetition to get a message across. Dynamic organizations do the same thing with their customers and their employees.

If you are a leader, repetition is your new best friend. If you are a parent, repetition is your new best friend. In both cases you are trying to communicate a message that is more complicated than "Drink Coke." This makes repetition even more important.

Now let's return to the theme of listening and connect how people hear what we communicate.

I'm amazed how often I will hear a leader say, "What's wrong with these people?"

"What do you mean?" I ask, already knowing where the conversation is going.

"I mean, I told them once. What do I need to do, hold their hands and make sure they do it? How many times do I need to tell them?"

"More than once, I guess," I say. They usually look at me with an expression somewhere between, "Why do I pay this idiot of the obvious to advise and consult me?" and "He'd better have more to contribute."

We have clearly established by now (I hope) that people need to be told more than once. What we have not covered sufficiently is *why*. Let me explain.

Imagine you are a leader sharing a message with your team.

The first time you tell someone something, chances are they are distracted or focused on something else. It takes time for them to focus, so they catch the end of your message and ignore it.

The second time you tell somebody something, they think to themselves, "This is his message for the week. He has a different message each week, and I'm really busy this week, so I'll get next week's message."

The third time you tell someone something, they ask a question, which makes you think they are engaged and listening. Wrong. They aren't interested in what you're saying yet. The reason for the question is they want to know how what you are saying is going to affect them—their role, their responsibilities, and their life. Remember, most people listen to the same radio station in their heads: WIIFM—what's in it for me?

The fourth time you tell somebody something, they think to themselves, "This must be really important, because this is the second time he is telling me this."

The fifth time you tell someone something, they ask another question and then listen to your answer with their question in mind to see if they believe you can be trusted.

The sixth time you tell somebody something, you have their attention for the first time and they really listen.

The seventh time you tell somebody something, they *might* actually hear it the way you were hoping it would be heard from the start.

Can the cycle be shortened? Sure. The more your team trusts you, the shorter the cycle. The healthier your culture, the shorter the cycle. A Dynamic Culture is a tree that bears fruit in every season and every situation.

A Good Plan Gives Everyone Priorities

The purpose of a Strategic Plan is to provide clarity around the mission and goals of an organization for a set period of time, usually one to three years.

A really good, *dynamic* Strategic Plan gives the whole organization clarity, direction, goals, and focus, if it is deployed correctly. Cascading the plan vertically and horizontally throughout the organization, from CEO to team leaders to front line employees in every department, helps each and every person understand how they can contribute to the success of the plan.

Every winning organization has mission and maintenance. Leaders of people who serve the mission in maintenance roles need to specifically and regularly reinforce the fact that the organization could not explore the next great opportunity if those people were not doing their roles and supporting the plan. All the work that goes into maintaining current systems and core offerings makes it possible for new opportunities to be explored. Ultimately this leads every person and every team to get very clear about what their priorities should be in order to ensure the success of the plan.

Every team member should be able to articulate what he or she is doing each day, week, month, quarter, and year to bring that plan to life. If they cannot, the probability of them accomplishing what is expected of them is close to zero.

Connect the dots. Show people how what they do helps the organization achieve its biggest goals this year and you get their attention in a new way. This type of clarity drives massive engagement among employees. Sharing the plan drives engagement. Priorities drive engagement. Transparency drives engagement. All four ignite trust—the corporate currency of our age—which in turn drives even greater engagement.

Systems Drive Behavior

What's the most powerful invention in history: the printing press, electricity, the automobile, the telephone, the internet, or something else? The question could be debated endlessly, but there is one answer that most people would overlook. Question: What do you call a farmer with a long stick? (I know it sounds like the beginning of a joke, but it isn't.) Answer: The inventor of leverage. And leverage is among the most powerful inventions in the history of the world.

One day a farmer was in the field and there was a huge rock in the middle of the field. He tried to lift it, but it quickly became clear that he was not going to be able. He tried to push it, but that turned out to be useless too. He stood there looking at the rock for a while, and then he had an idea. So he picked up a long stick, wedged it under the rock, applied pressure to the stick, and was able to move the rock. He invented leverage.

Leverage is one of the greatest inventions in history. We use it in thousands of ways every day to make our lives and work easier and more efficient. The six immutable principles of a Dynamic Culture are a form of leverage. They provide cultural leverage.

Systems are the great-grandchildren of leverage, maximizing it. Organizations everywhere leverage systems to maximize efficiency in so many ways, and we have become so used to them that we either don't even recognize them or we take them for granted. The leveraging power of systems is so great that some of the most successful organizations in the world have been built on them. Is McDonald's a business or a system? It's both. Can you make a better burger than McDonald's? Probably. I know I can. Can we make them in 100 countries, at 35,000 locations, serving 70 million customers a day? No, we can't. Like McDonald's, we would need more than a million employees and a highly refined system. Franchising is leverage. Franchising leverages a system to multiply what is possible on one corner in one city and makes it possible on corners in every city.

Simply measuring something is a system. What do you measure in your organization? Why do you measure it? When did you start measuring it? Does it still matter? What you measure sends a message. It tells your team these are the things that matter the most. Systems focus people. Is it important to measure things? Yes. But are you measuring the right things? Are you sending the right message and driving the behavior and outcomes you desire?

Systems are a form of communication, and a very powerful ally in the art of overcommunication. They are also one of your best friends when it comes to building a Dynamic Culture, creating clarity around mission, and empowering your organization to execute a Strategic Plan so effectively that they surprise themselves.

Organizations create systems and make changes to them all the time. What most leaders don't realize is that all change has both intended and unintended consequences. Politicians are particularly bad at foreseeing unintended consequences. Make a law that employers must provide health insurance for anyone who works 25 hours a week or more, and employers reduce employees to 20 hours a week and employ two people for 20 hours instead of one for 40 hours. So now the poor, rather than having one really average role and no health insurance, have two miserable roles and no health insurance. Those we tried to help actually got hurt because lawmakers didn't consider the unintended consequences.

The airlines decided they were going to charge people to check their bags. Intended consequence: the airlines make more money from people having to check bags. Unintended consequence: people bring everything they own on the plane as carry-on luggage, increasing the time it takes to board a plane; late departures skyrocket; and the experience of boarding a plane becomes more miserable than ever before.

Systems can be a very good thing, but you really need to think through all the consequences they will set in motion.

Another thing many leaders often fail to grasp is that there is a direct relationship between risk and reward. Decrease the reward and you decrease the risk people are willing to take. For a decade I worked with a Fortune 500 company where failure was so brutally dealt with that the culture developed a complete avoidance of risk. Because one failure basically meant the end of one's career, I suspect that all the best ideas never got voiced. Even the greatest minds in that organization kept their best ideas to themselves because the culture became completely risk averse. This is a huge problem. In all markets, risk and reward are directly related to each other. In a risk-averse culture people are more interested in not making a mistake than they are in coming up with the next great idea.

Compensation is a huge system. This is one area where many businesses forget the essentials. For example, business is a meritocracy, meaning if your products and services are good, customers will reward you by buying them and telling their friends about how amazing they are. If your goods and services are horrible, customers will punish you by *not* buying them, and they will tell their friends to avoid your business too. This is a basic meritocracy system. But when it comes to compensation, it's amazing how many organizations abandon the reality of meritocracy. If this is the system your customers use to give or take business from your organization, it's the best system to use to guide your compensation of employees.

Whom you reward, why you reward, and how to reward really matter, and will have a massive impact on the way people behave. It's a powerful system. If you have any doubt that systems drive behavior, make some changes to your compensation plan, then sit back and see what happens.

Take sales commissions as an example. How many salespeople promise the customer something they know is not possible just to get the sale (and their commission), leaving the inflated expectations and broken promise for the project to deal with? Be careful what you reward, because whatever you choose will be focused on at the expense of other things that may very well need your team's focus.

Culture is a system. Systems either empower or entitle people. The second is very bad for your organization, and is actually a form of violence against the dignity of people and one of the most common forms of organizational cancer.

When systems are at their best, they add value in ways that work twenty-four hours a day, seven days a week, 365 days a year. The beauty of good systems is that they always manage and monitor, so you don't have to be working all the time.

Leaders who don't leverage systems become unpredictable micromanagers who drive everyone around them crazy. It's like trying to play tennis and not knowing what the rules are.

Beloved leaders hire talented people and trust them to deliver on the plan, making themselves available to advise, consult, and pitch in as needed.

First thing every Monday morning, I have each of my direct reports email me the three most important things they will be working on that week. It's a very simple but powerful system, and the benefits are endless. Those emails tell me what my team is focused on for the week and where they might need my help or counsel. If I have a new direct report it allows me to learn how she prioritizes her work. If her priorities are not aligned with the mission, values, and Strategic Plan, I learn quickly and can coach her toward alignment.

Sometimes I see something on someone's list and can say, "Hey, keep this in mind when you are talking to . . ." or "I already took care of that." Sometimes the scope of a client's project changes over the weekend. One of my direct reports lists the project as one of her top three priorities, which immediately reminds me to shoot her a quick email or stop by her office for five minutes to update her so she doesn't waste time on the aspects of the project that have changed.

Three things on Monday morning—it's a super-simple system that helps the whole team get focused on the right things for the week, and allows a leader to correct course if necessary. Just as a Strategic Plan clarifies the priorities of an organization for a year or more, something as simple as these weekly emails clarifies priorities for individuals and teams—and clarity leads to impactful action and the optimum use of resources.

Then there are the dreaded meetings. When's the last time you were looking forward to attending a meeting—especially a regular one?

Meetings are systems. Most meetings are a horrible waste of

collective time. They are poorly planned and poorly executed, most people don't come prepared for them, and too many people see them as a break or a chance to catch up on their email (which is a myth unto itself; you are never going to catch up on your email). Hold regular meetings that are a waste of time and what message do you send people? It's OK to waste time here. A sense of urgency is one of my favorite qualities in all the best people I have ever hired, but once you extract that, you have set them on the long road to the mediocre middle.

If there is one thing your best people hate, it's when you waste their time. Do it often enough—with unnecessary meetings or anything else—and they will start looking for opportunities to add value elsewhere. Right, your best people don't look for *jobs*. They look for the best opportunity to engage their unique ability to add the most value to some great mission.

Not all systems are good. Meetings are a system. They can be a positive or a negative system. What do we call a system that has strayed from common sense and is rampant with other dysfunctions such as taking forever to make decisions? Bureaucracy.

Systems that don't increase mission impact frustrate your people.

Systems are essential for a well-executed Strategic Plan. The more of the Strategic Plan that is driven by or linked to good systems, the better chance you have of success. I've seen too many organizations whose own systems sabotage their new Strategic Plan; the plan is doomed from the start. So, once you have your Strategic Plan, it's time to review your current systems and consider: Will these systems empower people to accomplish your Strategic Plan? What are your best and worst systems? Do you have systems that encourage behavior that is counterproductive to your Strategic Plan and mission? Do you even know the type of behavior you are trying to encourage? Are your systems working for or against your Strategic Plan? Which of your systems damage your culture?

Develop a great Strategic Plan, employ the right people to work the plan, put the right systems and processes in place, and then hold people accountable. These are the keys to the powerful execution of your organization's Strategic Plan.

Systems are everywhere, and Dynamic Cultures harness the power of systems to create extreme competitive advantage and increase profits. That competitive advantage and increase in profit lead to a bigger future for everyone. Dysfunctional cultures end up costing a lot of money and creating even more human misery.

A business with a healthy culture is significantly more profitable than one with an unhealthy culture. It pays in dozens of ways to invest in Dynamic Culture, but the first investment you need to make is in your mind. I don't care if you are the receptionist or the CEO, or anyone in between, decide right now that a Dynamic Culture is possible where you work. Become a Culture Advocate today—do one thing, however small, to make your culture healthier today than it was yesterday.

Systems are at the center of almost everything we do to serve our customers. They are a good culture's best friend and a bad culture's worst enemy. One of the essential laws of organizational life is that *systems drive behavior*. This plays out in a thousand ways every day in every organization. Most of the time we don't recognize it happening. Open your eyes. Stop focusing on trying to change or correct the behavior; this is an exercise in futility. Identify the system that is creating the unwanted behavior and reengineer the system. Systems drive behavior.

The Success Trap

The most underrated singer-songwriter-musician in the world today, in my opinion, is Colin Hay. Born in Scotland, he moved to Australia as a child and, with his band Men at Work, became legendary for the song "Down Under," which has basically become the unofficial Aussie national anthem: "I come from the land down under . . ."

He has a Grammy and has sold millions of albums, his songs have appeared in dozens of movies and television shows, and he's writing and singing better than ever before. Like a fine wine stored in oak barrels for a dozen years or more, his voice gets richer every year. His lyrics reach from the very serious and profound to the humorous, and he is one of the few artists who can actually put two sentences together between songs to explain the origin of a song. In fact, I'd love to hear him give a commencement speech and see him write a book. And yet in a world of artificial talent and manufactured celebrity, there seems little room for someone as authentic as Colin Hay. He is an absolute giant in a world of midget pretenders.

You have great singers. You have great songwriters. You have great musicians. It is incredibly rare that someone is world-class at even two of the three. Most tend to be very strong at one and then limp along at one of the others. Colin is world-class at all three, and it is impossible to put into words how very rare that is.

Anyway, he was touring recently and I went to see him play a couple of times. He has an album called *Next Year People*, a title that we can apply to the business world: There is a danger that as Strategic Planners we will become next-year people, always planning for next year rather than making something happen this year.

But the reason for the story is a line from one of the songs on the album that makes very clear one of the major risks to even the best Strategic Plans. The song is called "If I Had Been a Better Man," and it is about a musician who rose to the very heights of stardom, who is now trying to make peace with some of the things he did, good and bad, to get to the top. There is one line from the song that is so pertinent to our conversation about planning: "I was mesmerized by shiny things." It happens all the time. As human beings, we get mesmerized by shiny things. It happens in relationships and careers, and it happens to organizations. They make the effort and spend the time to put together a solid Strategic Plan, but then they get distracted and mesmerized by shiny things.

Don't let that happen. The irresistible opportunity is the success trap. To stay focused and disciplined, sometimes you need to resist the irresistible. The problem is, people and organizations spend their whole lives trying to become successful and looking for great opportunities. Once you get a little bit successful, suddenly the ideas and opportunities come looking for you. Now there are more ideas and opportunities than could possibly be pursued. And the more successful you become, the more really good ideas and opportunities come your way. That's the problem. The success trap is *too many good opportunities*. All of those opportunities are a distraction. Focus on the plan.

If you want to be very successful as a parent, friend, spouse, mentor, leader, or anything worthwhile on the planet, get good at saying no. Don't say it in a dismissive way; learn to say it with empathy. But get very, very good at it. Everyone in your organization has to develop the discipline to say no, or at the very least, "Not now."

That said, I have come to what I am suggesting here only by doing it very badly for at least a decade after my first *New York Times* bestseller: *The only way to say no to anything is to have a deeper yes.* If you really want to save some money, find a deeper yes. Would you rather buy things that will be irrelevant a year from now or have a little more financial security and freedom? This applies to every area of life. Would you rather have that burger and fries right now or be alive to walk your daughter down the aisle on her wedding day? You get to decide.

Your Strategic Plan is your deeper yes; that's why you need to refer to it often. The way you convince yourself to say no to the latest shiny thing that you (or your team) have become mesmerized by is to realize that you aren't actually saying no to the shiny thing, you are saying yes to the very well-thought-out Strategic Plan that you are in the midst of executing right now.

Keep in mind, it's easy to say no to bad ideas. If you are successful it is relatively easy to say no to average things. The problem is, it's really hard to say no to good things. It is hard to say no to good ideas, and very, very hard to say no to great ideas.

Write down the shiny thing that mesmerizes you. Bring it to next year's strategic planning session and measure it against all the other ideas. You see, the real problem with these mesmerizing shiny things is that we consider them in isolation. Most ideas seem pretty good by themselves. But put that shiny idea next to ten other shiny ideas that have filtered up through the organization over the past twelve months and we will see just how good it really is.

New ideas can be one of the biggest distractions in any organization. If a leader has direct reports coming to her all the time with new ideas about what the team or organization should do, she will never get any work done. If you have a good strategy, focus on it. Ideas can be huge time wasters. The chances of a team member coming up with a big idea that trumps something that is already part of the Strategic Plan is extremely small, perhaps less than 1 percent.

If you can see small ways to improve efficiency and outcomes, that's different. Your leader is there to help you identify and implement these. How can you tell the difference? If something requires a shift in strategy, there is a high likelihood that it belongs to a once-a-year conversation rather than a passing conversation in the hallway or even a weekly huddle.

The truth is that if you have a well-considered Strategic Plan, there will not be much room for big, new ideas. Small tweaks can be made regularly to every role and team, but it's best to avoid the distraction of big, new ideas. Culture Advocates keep an ideas book. They write down the ideas that come to them over a period of time. Great leaders ask the organization for ideas before they update the Strategic Plan each year.

Give all your new employees an idea book as part of the onboarding process and explain that once a year they will be asked to present their ideas. Keep one yourself instead of bugging your leader every five minutes with new ideas.

We just got to the end of the first year of implementing this concept with a client for the first time. They have eighty-two employees who submitted around four hundred ideas. From those four hundred ideas, only one was selected to be added to the Strategic Plan and pursued; two others were already in development secretly in the upper echelons of the organization.

Life is choices. Business is choices. In both, we are constantly required to allocate scarce resources. There is only so much time, money, people, and so on. You cannot play golf and tennis on Saturday afternoon at the same time. You have to choose.

You might really like two cars, but you probably can't buy them both; you certainly can't drive them both at the same time. You have to decide. The reality is, every time you say yes to something you say no to *everything else* in that instance.

A leader has to decide how best to allocate scarce resources, by deciding which ideas will bear the most fruit with the least effort. The best leaders allocate resources with strategic priorities and don't allow themselves to get mesmerized by shiny things. But it takes discipline—the discipline of saying no.

Don't take it personally. Most ideas are good ideas, but it is only the very few great ideas that make it to the Strategic Plan in truly exceptional organizations. Culture Advocates are mindful that all resources are scarce and should be employed for maximum mission impact.

Dynamic Cultures don't let themselves get distracted with discussions about big, new ideas outside of certain times of the year. Until that time, people write them down in their idea book. Very rarely someone will have an idea that is so good and presents an opportunity that is so great, it cannot wait. These exceptions are usually easy to implement and have huge payoffs.

If you are good at anything, you are always going to have more opportunities than you can say yes to and stay healthy. That's true for people and organizations. I have learned this lesson the hard way too many times, both personally and professionally. It is a fierce mercy to encounter, but it will teach a powerful lesson if you listen.

Never forget that by saying no to something you are saying yes to what matters most: executing the mission in an excellent way. It doesn't need to be personal or emotional, although it will often feel that way; in reality, you are making sure you spend time and resources on what you have determined are your priorities.

This requires real clarity. Organizational clarity begins with mission. From there we move to the creation of a vibrant Strategic Plan. Then it is time to spread the word, to share the plan and the priorities within its pages. By helping each team member to develop clarity around his or her own priorities based on the organization's priorities, you give people the dignity of belonging to something bigger than themselves. From there it is simply a matter of consistently communicating and overcommunicating what matters most so that people can remember to focus their energy there each day, week, and month. Finally, beware of mesmerizing shiny things and the success trap. Dynamic Cultures are disciplined. They are good at saying yes and no to the right things, at the right times.

Make personal clarity a personal goal. Make professional clarity a professional (and organizational) goal. One of the greatest gifts this clarity of purpose provides is that it allows you to get really good at saying no, which most people and most organizations are really bad at.

But the best Strategic Plan in the world is useless if it is not followed by passionate and intentional action, so let's get busy. Measure your day against the plan. What percentage of today did you spend executing your organization's Strategic Plan? If we ask ourselves this question honestly at the end of each day, there will be many times when we are embarrassed. That's good. We should be.

We plan so we can act—and not just act, but act well and intentionally. Let the plan guide your action. Revisit the plan often. Don't just throw it in a drawer or put it on a shelf, like so many other Strategic Plans.

A Culture Advocate aligns more and more of his or her actions with the organization's mission, priorities, and plan every day. Mission Is King, and the Strategic Plan is the best way for the mission to be accomplished. It is, the Culture Advocate believes, the best way to ensure that the main thing remains the main thing.

Success brings with it new paradigms and problems. Most people and organizations only have to decide between good and bad opportunities. Now you have to choose between two good opportunities, or maybe two great opportunities, or even two amazing opportunities that you never in your life thought you would have a shot at. That's when your resolve gets tested. It is very hard to say no to great opportunities. Now you have to learn to be highly selective.

What happens if you don't? You poison the culture by overworking and overwhelming everyone; you grow too fast and don't have the systems, processes, and infrastructure in place; and the whole organization begins to buckle and crack under the weight and the pressure. It's not pretty. I've seen it a hundred times. Disciplined growth requires enormous character and is a very, very hard thing for most leaders to promote and hold their organization accountable to.

The thing about success is that it throws an unlimited number of opportunities at you. The success trap is having more opportunities than you can take advantage of. It's a blessing and a curse. Decide to let it be a blessing for you and your organization by having the discipline to say no.

Why Share the Plan?

Many leaders get nervous when I talk about sharing the plan below the team leader level. I get it. And I agree and disagree depending upon the situation. First, there is at least some summary of the Strategic Plan that should be shared with every member of the organization. In fact, if you want to get ingenious, share a copy of that summary with all your key partners, so they know what you are trying to accomplish and can help you. It will probably be the first time a supplier has had a customer give them a summary of their Strategic Plan and said, "Help us make this happen!" Why have your key external partners wandering around in the dark?

Why share the plan so widely? *Scientia potential est* is a Latin saying attributed to Sir Francis Bacon meaning "Knowledge is power." When it comes to sharing a Strategic Plan (or key elements of it) far and wide, knowledge is *empowerment.*

Knowledge of the plan gives people the clarity necessary to make solid decisions. Solid decisions lead to more mission-centric work, which is always going to be more effective and efficient. All of these factors lead to higher employee engagement and increased morale and profits, which lead to increased compensation and benefits, and in turn, to everything each leader should want for the organization.

If you don't tell your team where you are going, they can't help you get there. But tell them what you need, tell them where you are going, explain to them what you are trying to achieve—and that's when you discover what kind of team members they are.

Usability

A plane that doesn't fly is useless. A car that won't start is useless. A bike with flat tires is useless. We use all these things to get places. The role of a Strategic Plan is to get an organization somewhere.

Throughout this book I have been referring to a dynamic Strategic Plan. One of the key qualities of a dynamic Strategic Plan is its usability. How usable is it? For example, if it is nine hundred pages long, its sheer size makes it unusable. If it proposes four hundred goals of equal importance, this foolishness renders it useless.

When I first started writing books, I never thought about usability. I focused on the ideas I wanted to share with the reader. Today, realizing how busy people are, how little time they have to read, and how few people even read at all, I see that as an author it is my responsibility to write books that not only inspire and share great insights and ideas but also are easy for busy people to consume. Even more than that, it is my challenge to write books for people who don't usually read. There is nothing more satisfying than someone coming up to me and saying, "I never read, but I read your book from cover to cover," or "I have to be honest, your book is the first book I've read since high school."

But usability is something that most authors never even think about, and something I am certain is not taught in writing classes. Over the years I have realized that the usability of a book is just as important as the content. Most books I write go through four or five drafts before I feel they're right. But over the past five years or more, I have been taking the books through six, seven, even eight drafts, with the extra drafts focused almost exclusively on usability.

For example, the book you are reading right now began as an eight-chapter book. Eight long chapters, some of them really, really long. At the end of the second draft, I started thinking to myself, "I am going to lose too many people in chapter three; it is twice as long as the other chapters." Now you are holding a book made up of seven chapters, but divided into more than fifty sections so you can easily pick it up and set it down in the midst of your busy life. This usability eliminates the excuse that you don't have time to get into it today. You have time every day to read at least one section of this book. The large ideas in bold are specifically designed to ensure you don't miss key points, as well as to help you return to the book in the future and get a quick refresher. These sections also allow you to easily find ideas you want to share with other people.

Similarly, when you think you have finished writing your Strategic Plan, start thinking about how it is going to be used. If you do this seriously, you will discover you need *at least* one more draft to get it right. If you want to keep mission king, making your Strategic Plan usable is essential. How is each leader going to use the plan each week? How will leaders and their teams use it? How will individual contributors use the summary provided? Most businesses skip this step, which traditionally has been part of the strategic planning process.

Why don't organizations spend time considering how the Strategic Plan will be used and revise it accordingly? First, because it never occurred to them; second, even if it occurred to them, they wouldn't do it because too few people actually believe the Strategic Plan will be broadly used. The final version of a Strategic Plan should be simple, focused, practical, and eminently usable.

I think when I was younger I just wanted people to buy my books. It wasn't so much about the money as it was about the validation of both my work and my ego. I was insecure, like all of us, and I needed some affirmation in this path. As I got older, I became more interested in people *reading* the books than I was in having another bestseller. But now I want more—I want to write books that transform people, their lives, and their businesses. I have found that making books practical, helpful, hopeful, and generally usable is the key to making this happen.

Nobody's going to buy a copy of your Strategic Plan; it won't make a bestseller list. You have a different choice: Do you want to print and bind it very neatly? Do you just want people to read it? Or do you want people to *live* it? The latter, I hope, so let's continue our discussion about how you make your organization's Strategic Plan a living, breathing document that is constantly referred to for priorities, decisions, and inspiration.

What's Your Role in All This?

A Culture Advocate automatically asks herself: What can I do today to help this organization become a-better-version-of-itself and accomplish its mission as stated in the Strategic Plan? A Culture Advocate doesn't wait to be asked or told to do something; she just gets busy and makes stuff happen.

Get really clear about what you and your team are being asked to accomplish. Highlight the parts that apply directly to you—then get busy crushing those things. Underline the parts that apply directly to your team—then get busy crushing those things, even if you are not directly responsible for some parts. Jump in and help where you can. Treat people like people. If you know a teammate has a sick child at home, offer to help for a couple of hours so he can leave early and get home to his child.

Decide today: Do you want to be a babysitter or a parent? The babysitter's role is basically to ensure the child does not die while the parents are out to dinner. But the parent's role is infinitely more complex, dealing with issues like health, education, religion, and extracurricular involvement. Parents are responsible for the development of the whole person—their child.

As the owner of a number of businesses, I have come to the conclusion over the years that either people don't see the things I see, or they see them but don't care. When I walk into an organization I own or lead, I tend to see the scratches on the wall, delivery boxes stacked on expensive furniture, stains on the carpet, trash on the floor. Most were probably the result of carelessness, and most of them would not be there if this were those people's homes.

Owners see things that others don't see. Become an owner. Think like an owner and ask yourself, "What would she see that I am not seeing?" Do this and your awareness will go off the charts—you will start seeing things that most people don't. You might not own the business, but you own some part of that plan. This is your sweet spot. This is where you can have the most impact. Own it. Dominate it. Crush it. Knock it out of the ballpark.

We will talk about the role of a leader (formerly known as a manager) in a moment, but the role of an employee is to execute the organization's priorities in a timely and efficient way. A practical Strategic Plan brings the power of clarity to every person in the organization. This will have a huge impact on the efficiency, effectiveness, and outcomes of every person and team.

Think about those last two sentences. It's easy to just read through them without pausing to think about what they're saying. We underestimate the power of clear expectations. That's why we don't take the time to establish them, either personally or professionally. Now let's read those lines again: *A practical Strategic Plan brings the power of clarity to every person in the organization. This will have a huge impact on the efficiency, effectiveness, and outcomes of every person and team.*

Lesson: Clarity is incredibly powerful, and most people lack it when it comes to their role and especially the whole organization's priorities.

You, the employee, need to get clear about what your leader expects of you. Don't be surprised if he doesn't know the first time you ask him. Expect something like, "You're doing great, John, just keep doing what you're doing." That's OK for round one. But then you need to request some time to discuss. That's round two. It will take a few rounds. We will cover this in much more depth a little later. The point is, if you don't know what is expected of you, how can you deliver on it and exceed it?

The work you do creates a chain reaction throughout the organization. It impacts lives—the customer experience; everyone's pay and benefits packages next year—and in some cases, it could be a life-or-death experience. If you are lazy, do bad work, and treat customers poorly, you are punishing yourself and your colleagues, because you and they will make less money next year. There is no simpler way to say it. And, of course, if this goes on long enough and enough people adopt the same attitude, the organization will cease to exist and everyone will lose their employment.

Do What You Can Where You Are Now

In a world where instant gratification isn't fast enough anymore, describing our society as impatient is an understatement of monumental proportions. The desire to do more, have more, and advance faster has outpaced any generation of the past. What is missing is the desire to be and become more. Who you become is infinitely more important than what you do or have. Speeding up many of life's natural processes often ends in disaster. How many people do you know who inherited a fortune? Do you think they really became who they were capable of becoming or intended to become? Probably not—and the reason is quite simple. When someone builds wealth in an ethical way, he or she develops character just by going through the process. When parents give their children the wealth, they cannot also give them the character that was developed by amassing that wealth.

Wherever you are in your career, wherever you are in your organization right now, don't despise these times. These are times for becoming, time for learning to be the-very-best-version-of-yourself, so that as more opportunity and responsibility come your way, you are prepared to succeed.

Sometimes it can seem mundane or boring, or even beneath us. Culture Advocates are humble. They find joy in whatever they are doing. I recently sat next to a man on a plane who worked for Delta Air Lines. I asked him what he did, and he explained that he worked in plane maintenance. We talked a bit about it and then I said, "Everyone has bad days, right? What do you do to ensure you don't make a mistake when you are having a bad day?" Three things, he said. "First, I just focus on what is in front of me right now. Second, I always—good day or bad day—remind myself that my kids fly on these planes; my wife, my parents, my friends, and everyone I love flies on these planes. But remembering that my own children fly on these planes brings a real focus. The third thing I do if I'm having a bad day is check my work even more than I usually would.

Then of course the organization has systems and processes in place to ensure the work is done, done properly, and checked." Wow. Talk about an unexpected, inspiring conversation.

"Do what you can, with what you have, where you are," was the counsel of Theodore Roosevelt. Francis of Assisi, one of the few spiritual figures in history to be loved and respected by men and women of all faiths and no faith, wrote, "Begin by doing what is necessary; then do what is possible; and suddenly you will find yourself doing the impossible."

We all want the next step faster, but the fastest way to get it is to passionately embrace whatever is before you right now and crush it.

A Team Leader's Role

If you are a team leader of any type, you have a unique role to play when it comes to ensuring the Strategic Plan gets executed successfully. Your knowledge of the plan could be the difference between your own team's success or failure, and that could be the difference between the organization's success or failure. This is why it is essential that you know which parts of the plan matter most to your team. Refer to them often in meetings and conversations; highlight, underline, and dog-ear them in your copy of the plan. And carry the plan with you almost everywhere you go.

This is the heart of the issue: A day should never pass without some reference to the plan. Your knowledge of the plan will be used in a number of ways. First, to bring clarity to the whole team about their role in accomplishing the organization's priorities. Next, if you are a leader, it is your responsibility to connect the dots between the mission and the Strategic Plan and each team member's role. Remember, the mission is unchanging and the Strategic Plan is just the way the organization has chosen to accomplish its mission right now. It will change.

Ask people how their daily work impacts the plan. If they don't know, explain it. Culture Advocates are always trying to get clear about their own role, as well as helping others get clear about their roles. Role clarity is one of the central pieces of building and sustaining a Dynamic Culture.

"But what if the dots don't connect?" I get this question a lot. "I work in the accounting department and there is no priority in that new Strategic Plan that impacts my role or department." This may appear to be true sometimes, but it never is, and a seasoned leader of people cannot fall into this trap. It is a morale killer and a creator of subcultures (which are a disease unto themselves).

As an organization grows, there is a certain amount of maintenance that needs to be done to push the mission forward. That maintenance work is essential, but it doesn't always feel essential to the people doing it. It doesn't come with huge accolades and is often unappreciated. Although if, for example, you were the payroll person, if you didn't pay people next pay period, I suspect they would be reminded of the essential nature of your role quickly.

The leader of a team that deals with maintenance aspects of the mission needs to pay special attention to reminding each person how their role supports the great priorities set out in the Strategic Plan. The leader also needs to benchmark performance, encourage continuous learning and improvement, and generally drive ever greater efficiency in all these areas.

Every team member needs and deserves context. They need to know how the work they do connects with the mission, direction, strategy, and end goal of the organization. They need (and want) to know how they can contribute to the organization's success. Most people don't want to do less. Yes, there are minimalists who are always asking, "What's the least I can do?" But they don't tend to last long in a Dynamic Culture. Most people want to do more. But they want to do more of the stuff that will have the most impact.

A leader's role is to ensure that every person on her team has everything he or she needs to add as much value as possible. One part of that is clarity around where they fit into the plan and how they contribute to the mission. It is not enough to tell your team this once. Like any important message, it needs to be overcommunicated.

You are responsible for the formal and informal dissemination of your organization's Strategic Plan among your team members. When was the last time you looked at it? How often do you look at it? How often do you refer to it in meetings or in discussions with your team?

Rule No. 1 of Overcommunication

My friend Mark has had an amazing career in business, but more important, he is the kind of person who gets fulfillment and joy from mentoring others to succeed. He has taught me much, but there are two things he has taught me that I think about at least once a week. The first: Organize around the work. Not to do so is a mistake that so many organizations make, and it causes inefficiency, frustration, and failure. For example, many people will put together org charts with no regard for how work flows through the organization. In a factory, each worker should have the tools he or she uses the most the closest, and those he or she uses the least farthest away. Think about your own work space—is it set up this way? Think about your kitchen at home—is it set up this way? Organize around the work.

The second lesson Mark has taught me is what I want to discuss here: What's clear to me is not necessarily clear to you. Our assumption when we speak is that people understand what we are saying, and it is almost never true. Every person hears what we say through the filter of their own thoughts, experiences, biases, prejudices, blind spots, and the mood they are in that day.

Speaking to groups, I am sometimes amazed in conversations after a presentation to learn what some people think I said. What's clear to me is not necessarily clear to you, or anybody else. *Do not assume that people understand what you are saying, especially the first time you tell them.*

This is why one of the central premises of overcommunication is dialogue. Overcommunication isn't just about telling people something over and over again. That's only one piece of it. It is also about helping people understand how, where, and why they fit into the team and the plan. But don't just tell people something—ask them what they heard. You'll be surprised, amazed, disappointed, and even discouraged sometimes, but at least you will know what you are dealing with. And once you know that, you will know two things for sure: What's clear to you is not necessarily clear to another person; and it is impossible to overestimate the importance of overcommunication.

Culture might eat strategy for breakfast, but I wouldn't want to lead an organization that didn't have a well-developed Strategic Plan. If you've got one, dust it off and start using it. If you don't have one, it might be time to start thinking about developing one.

Wherever you are in the process, there is one essential truth when it comes to empowering people to accomplish anything: People don't do anything until they are inspired, but once they are inspired, there is almost nothing they will not do.

In 1963, Martin Luther King Jr. didn't stand on the steps of the Lincoln Memorial and say, "I have a Strategic Plan." Sure, he had one, but that's not what he said. He said, "I have a dream," and captured the imagination of the whole nation. The message resonated with even those who hated him, because we all have dreams. Our dreams animate us and bring us to life—they energize us, focus us, bring meaning to even the simplest tasks, and make everything new, fresh, and fun.

Great cultures inspire their people. They do it in dozens of ways, formally and informally, and together they keep the dream of the mission alive. They do this by harnessing the third immutable principle of Dynamic Cultures: They overcommunicate the plan.

The Third Principle:
OVERCOMMUNICATE THE PLAN

it all starts with hiring

Why Are Most Organizations Bad at Hiring?

Let me begin this chapter with a warning and a reminder. The warning first: If you are not a leader, it would be a mistake to think you can skip this chapter because hiring doesn't impact you. Every person your organization hires impacts your salary, the quality of your benefits package, and your work environment. Everyone should be deeply interested in hiring for these reasons alone, but we are just getting started.

Now, a reminder: I promised you a book that every person in an organization should read and will hopefully benefit from tremendously. And I closed the section where I identified the promise of this book by reiterating my hope that the ideas in these pages would reach deep into both your personal and professional lives. Here we find a perfect example.

Even if the preceding warning were not true or relevant to you in any way, the truth is that we all hire people to do different things in our lives. Want to sell your house? You need to hire a Realtor. Want to put together a financial plan? You need to hire a great life coach or financial adviser. Have you ever called someone to do something like paint your house? You were hiring. Going to a restaurant for lunch today? You are actually hiring people to cook for you and serve you. The list is endless.

We are all hiring people all the time. If you really want to learn about an organization, offer to help with the Hiring Process. Offer to do the grunt work of reviewing and scoring résumés or screening candidates. A very unique power and influence surrounds hiring, and most people overlook it. If you said to me, "Matthew, we want you to change this culture but you can only be in charge of one thing," I'd choose hiring. Depending on a number of factors, it may take a long time to transform the culture, but you can do it with this single lever.

Tragically, this area of organizational life is typically ignored. Worse, it is often seen as a nuisance. Most organizations are bad at hiring for at least one of these five reasons:

1. They don't have a hiring plan.
2. Their hiring plan is inadequate or flawed.
3. They ignore their hiring plan and lack any hiring discipline.
4. Their leaders don't take hiring seriously.
5. The wrong person is in charge of hiring.

The truth is, I am a convert to the power and importance of a really good Hiring Process. For twenty years I was making all the same mistakes everyone else was making, until a couple of guys working with me at an organization I was leading cornered me one day. They asked for fifteen minutes to talk about hiring, and I very reluctantly agreed. Those fifteen minutes changed my life. This particular organization was in the midst of massive growth; we had twenty open positions, and the best way to describe our Hiring Process was chaos.

Andrew Krumme and George Josten made me believe in the importance of an organization's Hiring Process. In fact, show me your Hiring Process and I can probably tell you what the culture is like at your organization; I can probably even predict the future of your organization. And much of what I will share with you in this chapter we all learned together on the journey that followed that fifteen-minute meeting three years ago.

The Top 10 Hiring Mistakes

The reality is organizations make so many hiring mistakes that I could probably make an entire Top 100 list, but we will stick to the following ten simply to give context to the rest of the conversation.

1. Not being crystal clear on what you want a person to accomplish in a role. This needs to be defined well before even posting the role. And it's probably not a bad idea to work out why the last person in the role left.

2. Focusing too much on filling the position rather than ensuring you find the right person; hiring simply to fill a position rather than to reinforce your organization's culture.

3. Asking the wrong questions, talking too much, and failing to let the candidate speak, even if that means waiting through those long, awkward silences.
4. Hiring the best candidate from a pool. The whole pool of candidates might be B or C players, so even if you hire the best in the pool, you still get a B player. Sometimes you need to start over and get a whole new pool of candidates.
5. First-impression bias.
6. Neglecting to call references.
7. Hiring someone for the wrong reasons, such as doing a favor for somebody else.
8. No consistent interview process.
9. Failure to adequately prepare other team members who will be interviewing the candidate.
10. Hiring someone from the outside when someone inside the organization would be a much better fit.

Experience has shown me that less than 5 percent of organizations are really good at hiring people. Culture Advocates are hungry to see the right people with the right skills, experience, and attitude join the team. If you do not have a Hiring Process, you will fail. I will help you put one together here soon.

As I was growing up in Australia, my childhood was filled with cricket. My seven brothers and I were obsessed with the sport. Every family gathering involved a very serious cricket match, and most ended in some sort of brawl. In cricket, a batsman is taught what great baseball batters are taught in baseball: Wait for your pitch.

The same is true when it comes to hiring. The essence of a good Hiring Process is patience: Start patient, remain patient, and stay patient even when people are pressuring you to hire the wrong person for a role. The right candidate will come along, but you have to wait. Don't swing at everything.

Hire from a position of strength. You don't want to feel like you are reaching too far for a pitch, because the farther you have to reach, the weaker your swing becomes. When you hire from a position of weakness, it usually ends up being a mistake. And never, ever hire out of desperation. Contract someone to help fill a gap, but never hire a permanent team member out of desperation. That is a recipe for disaster. And let's be clear, a disaster is very different from a mistake. This is why you can never let someone who is desperate to fill a role control the Hiring Process; a great Hiring Process has checks and balances.

It may seem a little old-fashioned or overused, but successful hiring is all about going the extra mile. The interesting thing is that there are tons of old-fashioned things that still work amazingly well today, while plenty of new stuff breaks in five minutes.

I posed a question earlier: Why are most organizations bad at hiring? I've never had anyone challenge the assumption of the question. I suspect this is because deep down we all know it's true. Culture Advocates are passionate about changing this. But to answer the question, the reason most organizations are bad at hiring is because they are lazy and they have no process. This lack of process leads to a lack of discipline and a swing-at-every-pitch attitude, which is always a failing strategy.

Most organizations are bad at hiring because they are lazy. Hiring is hard work. It is an incredibly difficult thing to do and especially to do really well. And it is only going to get harder, because employee quality is diminishing as people's lives become more dysfunctional. So if you want to get really good at this—individually, as a team, or as an organization—get ready to roll up your sleeves and work hard at mastering it.

There are no shortcuts when it comes to getting good at hiring, either as an individual or as an organization. You just have to go the hard yards. It's obvious in a sense, but common sense is more and more uncommon every day. I am reminded of something I once heard Coach John Wooden say: "Why is it so hard for so many people to realize that it is usually those that work harder and longer that end up succeeding?"

There has been a lot of talk about game changers in many spheres over the past ten years, but little talk about organizational game changers. Establishing and implementing the right Hiring Process will be a massive game changer for your organization.

If you don't have a great Hiring Process, I am so excited for you. It has been one of the most satisfying experiences of my career as a business consultant to go with my team into organizations, help them develop a Hiring Process, and then get to watch as they implement it. Let's talk about where you are right now and the skills you need to develop a fabulous Hiring Process.

The first step is always to get very clear about what you are looking for in each candidate.

The Three Things

Ask any business owner if he or she would like to hire two more rainmakers, and most likely they will say, "No, I'd like to hire six more rainmakers." If you look up *rainmaker* in most dictionaries you will find two definitions:

1. Someone who makes it rain using either rituals or scientific methods.
2. A person who generates revenue for a business by attracting new clients and brokering new deals.

Ask your sales team leader how many rainmakers she would like to hire and she will likely say, "As many as I can get my hands on." Lots of people claim to be rainmakers in the interview process, but rainmakers are very hard to find. If you dissect a big deal in the interview process, you will most likely discover that the interviewee wasn't actually the rainmaker; he was the wingman. There's nothing wrong with that, but wingmen are easy to find.

Two things amaze me: how few people know if they are looking for a rainmaker or a wingman, and how many people hire a wingman hoping he will become a rainmaker. Wingmen rarely become rainmakers. In fact, I've never seen it happen. Rainmakers usually have a long history of making it rain. They didn't wake up at age thirty-five, forty-five, or fifty-five and discover they have this hidden talent. People don't change that much, usually. Some will sit in interviews and say they have never had the opportunity to be a rainmaker, and given the chance they will make it rain like the best of them. But rainmakers have something in common with Culture Advocates when it comes to opportunities: They don't wait for them to come along; they make them happen.

Sometimes it takes creative questions to get really clear about who and what you are looking for in a particular role. One of my favorites is: Are we looking for a babysitter or a parent? The two roles are very different; we all know that. Remember, a babysitter doesn't have to worry about what school to send the child to or make sure the child is getting a balanced diet and enough exercise. A babysitter doesn't have to make sure the child is up-to-date on tetanus and other vaccinations in case the child steps on a rusty nail. A babysitter is essentially responsible for keeping the child alive and ensuring the house doesn't burn down.

A parent, on the other hand, is responsible for everything—the physical, emotional, intellectual, and spiritual development of their child. This leads to dozens of questions every week. It requires a parenting philosophy and ownership of outcomes.

When it comes to filling an open position at work, sometimes you just need a babysitter, but other times you need a parent. If you need a parent and you hire a babysitter, you are going to have a problem.

But the point isn't about rainmakers, though that is a good lesson for us all to learn. And it is not about babysitters and parents, but that's also a helpful analogy in the Hiring Process. The point is, knowing who and what you are looking for is critical to the process of hiring the right people for your organization.

There are two exercises that I enjoy doing with leaders and employees. The first poses a question to employees: If you could determine your personal brand by being known by everyone in the organization for three qualities, what would they be? The second poses a question to leaders: If you could magically infuse all your employees with three qualities, what would they be?

The employee exercise is designed to help individuals think about and define how they want to be perceived within the organization. It is essentially a personal branding exercise.

The leadership exercise is designed to help leaders think about and define what breed of team member they are trying to raise up. Identifying the three qualities leaders would like to see in their employees gives leaders something to anchor their comments on any topic to, and that is just one of a thousand ways they serve an organization.

One way for leaders to develop an amazing team is to consider these questions: What does a great employee look like? What do you expect of them? Who has been successful in this organization in the past? What made them successful? Who is successful in the organization today? Who founded the organization? What qualities do they have in common? Who do you really enjoy working with and why? But there are a dozen ways to approach the exercise.

Every time I do one of these exercises, I get asked the same question: What are your three? To which I always respond, "I will tell you when we are finished with the exercise."

So, what are the three qualities I look for in people? Committed, coachable, and aware. They are what I try to develop in team members. But first and foremost, they are what I try to foster in myself.

Committed. When you interview someone for a role, you can't really tell if they will commit to the role or to your organization. They don't really know the role or the culture. But you can explore what they have committed to in the past, and you can get a sense of someone's commitment muscles. The good news is you can do a lot to influence a new employee's commitment to their role and to the organization. But at some point, commitment becomes binary—zeros and ones. You can't be a little bit committed. You either are or you aren't.

Coachable. Coachability is one of the leading indicators of success at anything. Give me someone with a strong work ethic, a reasonable intellect, a positive attitude, and coachability and we will do great things together. Champions love being coached, because they are hungry to get better every day and they know that ultimately victory comes down to seconds and inches. When you interview someone, you probe their history, exploring the best coaches, mentors, teachers, and leaders they have worked with throughout their life. But then you need to ask the candidate to tell you about the worst coaches, mentors, teachers, and leaders they have encountered in life. This is the real question. Everyone thinks they are coachable; but we are all resistant to coaching sometimes. The desire to learn and get better is a sign of hunger for excellence. A rigid desire to do things our own way (or the way they have always been done) is a sure sign of mediocrity. A coaching culture is a Dynamic Culture.

Aware. Are you aware of how what you are doing and saying is affecting the people around you? Do you notice when someone isn't quite herself? I have two great assistants. They are proactive; most of the time I don't even need to ask for things, because they are already aware of my needs. Are you aware of your children's needs, your leader's needs, your lover's needs? Are you curious about people and their stories? On the flip side, people who completely lack any sense of awareness frustrate us massively. We hear a lot of talk about emotional intelligence (EQ), but ask most people to give you an example of it and they can't. Awareness is an everyday, living, breathing example of EQ. Are you aware when people are and are not listening to you? Do you engage people with questions to ensure they comprehend what you are saying? Do you practice active listening, repeating back to people, "So, what I hear you telling me is . . ." to make sure you comprehend what they are trying to tell you? Awareness is one of the highest forms of emotional intelligence.

Knowing who and what you are looking for in a candidate (and every member of your team) is essential to successful hiring.

Another thing to consider is mind-set and disposition. We live in a world of rapid change—so rapid that many organizations and employees are constantly in catch-up mode. We never get caught up. When was the last time you sat at your desk with a deep sense of satisfaction and thought to yourself, "I'm all caught up!" Not going to happen. We also live in a culture where instant gratification isn't quick enough. So if you are looking for someone to perform a role that requires patience, it's important to be mindful of the cultural pool you are fishing in and to be sure to find a candidate who has a track record of patience. It will be the guy who took care of his dying grandfather for five years. You have to get beyond the surface and discover the events that formed a person and her life in order to really know a candidate.

Rapid change has brought with it constant transition. Our lives and our businesses are perpetually in a transition of some type, and different people respond to change in different ways. You have innovators—they love change, because they dreamed it up. You have early adopters, who are comfortable with uncertainty, so they are excited to see where this train is going and jump on board quickly. Then you have the mass middle, the people who keep their heads down and do their work and leave it to leadership to decide where the train should be going. Some people are always late; they are the late adopters, who realize the train is leaving with or without them, so they jump on. Finally, you have a very dangerous group of people, the resisters and the saboteurs. Resisters disagree with the new plan; saboteurs are just jaded and cynical and no matter what the plan is, they will try to sabotage it. It is important to be ever mindful that there are different types of people, and to continually look for fresh ways to explore their differences.

This ties in to another important point: Once you know who you are looking for, it's time to go out and find them. Let me start by saying, where you fish matters! You are unlikely to find a Chinook salmon in the Ohio River. You could fish that river for ten years and never catch one. But suppose you need to find an early adopter to fill a role. You could include that when you post the role, and you probably should. Or you could look for a place where you know early adopters gather. Where can you find a whole bunch of early adopters in the same place, at the same time, on the same day? They line up outside Apple stores around the world every time the technology giant releases a new product. Get out there, walk the line, talk to people to find out what they do, and ask those who seem like potential candidates if they are interested in exploring a new opportunity.

People don't want jobs; they want careers. They want opportunities to use and develop their talents. They want a chance to do something they can be passionate about.

Are you looking in the right places? It's time to find new ponds to fish.

The majority of people who apply for jobs don't have jobs, and it is important to explore why they don't have a job. The future of hiring belongs to people who are willing to get creative about finding great talent, and that means going out and finding it. Culture Advocates are always looking for talent in unexpected places. The people you really want to hire already have roles and are not looking for another opportunity.

Finding the right people to take your organization into the

richly imagined future is about attraction, not promotion. It is time to think about attracting talent in new and creative ways. A Dynamic Culture attracts talent. Culture Advocates attract talent. And a well-thought-out, disciplined Hiring Process will set you leaps and bounds ahead of your competition. So, as this section draws to a close, take a few minutes to reflect on these questions:

- Do you have a strategy for hiring great people?
- How good is your Hiring Process?
- When was the last time you thought of hiring as a competitive advantage?
- Do you hire the first people who come along or do you hire the very best person for each and every role?
- Are the people you are hiring this year better than the people you hired last year?
- How do the most talented people in your industry perceive your organization?
- Do you have a strategy to find great people for your organization? If not, are you ready to do something about it?

How Good Is Your Hiring Process?

The key to hiring employees is simple, right? Hire great people. The key to a great Hiring Process is also simple: Hire the right people. But simple is not the same as easy.

Directives such as "Hire great people" and "Hire the right people" sound insultingly straightforward and logical, even simple. And yet the anxiety and anguish that surround this aspect of business are almost impossible to overestimate. It is people problems that keep leaders awake at night, that ruin family dinners. Too many family dinners are ruined by someone complaining about a colleague or boss.

People problems dominate the conversation in the lunch-room, copy room, break room, in leadership meetings, and in the corridors of most businesses. People problems are one of the main causes of gossip, which is one of the most significant forms of culture cancer. It's tragic and true, but what makes it so difficult to swallow is that these people problems could have been completely avoided in 99 percent of cases if a dynamic Hiring Process had been in place.

Most organizations are bad at hiring because they lack dis-cipline and don't have a rigorous Hiring Process. How bad are they? Worse than they think, and much worse than most would ever admit if they really knew. This is perhaps the biggest undi-agnosed problem in most organizations.

Now, it's important to understand in the midst of what we are discussing here that hiring mistakes are *very* expensive—they may be the largest line item that doesn't show up on your profit and loss statement. Not only are they expensive finan-cially, but they are expensive for the culture, and that is the real currency when it comes to attracting, nurturing, and retaining talent. The point I am trying to make is that hiring mistakes are really expensive. Hiring mistakes may be the largest line item that doesn't show up on your profit and loss statement.

What percentage of organizations get it wrong when it comes to hiring?

- In 66 percent of cases, managers know within 30 days that they have made a hiring mistake. Most do nothing about it. They know they have hired the wrong person, but they can't be bothered to go through the whole process again.

- The first person to know you made a hiring mistake is usually the employee.
- More than 40 percent of your employees are likely looking for a role at another organization right now.
- Twenty-two percent of new hires leave their roles within 45 days of being hired, and 40 percent leave within 6 months.
- Of 2,000 managers who were interviewed, 33 percent indicated they know within the first 90 seconds if they will hire a candidate.
- Employers are facing the most serious shortage of talent ever, and the most talented prospects are much more interested in culture than they are in your benefits package. Seventy-two percent of CEOs are concerned about the availability of workers with key skills to fill key positions.
- American organizations spend $72 billion a year recruiting and hiring.
- Only 9 percent of senior managers believe turnover is a serious problem.
- The average cost to replace an employee making $10 an hour is $5,500.
- Less than 1 percent of organizations have developed or are strengthening their Hiring Process as a key objective in their current Strategic Plan.

Let's be very clear from the beginning. Get your hiring and onboarding process right and your chances of creating a Dynamic Culture increase exponentially.

So, how good is your Hiring Process? Give it a score between 1 and 10. Now halve that score and you are probably closer to the truth. If you are a leader and you are not really sure what your Hiring Process is, then you obviously don't know how good or bad it is, so you are just guessing, but more important, you are not paying attention to one of the most important aspects of leading your organization.

If you want to build a Dynamic Culture, the only place to start is with hiring. Most organizations are bad at hiring people, yet nothing is more important. Get this right and many other aspects of culture building will fall into place. Nothing will impact the culture and success of an organization more than the Hiring Process it adopts. Organizations rise or fall on their ability to attract, grow, nurture, and retain talent. Get hiring right and you will change the culture.

The Fourth Principle:
HIRE WITH RIGOROUS DISCIPLINE

I have made it clear that I think mission should be king in any organization. But if mission weren't king, the Hiring Process would be. It is *that* important.

What's the role of a Culture Advocate in the Hiring Process? Culture Advocates are talent magnets. They are always looking for talent in unexpected places. I'll let you in on a little secret: The best talent isn't in the places you'd expect to find it. One of my assistants didn't even apply for that role—she was applying online for a role as a nanny. I saw her résumé, interviewed her, told her she wasn't getting the role as a nanny, and offered her a career. She is amazing.

I'd hire the guy who handles checking my car in to be serviced. He has great people skills, is good at managing conflict, has great communication skills, and in a world where it is almost impossible to find great service, he delivers world-class service every time.

Culture Advocates are always out there looking for talent. Yes, it's good that people send us résumés and apply for roles, but there is something about their current situation that is causing them to do that—and half the time that "something" is them.

Start looking for talent in unexpected places. If you need people who wake up in the morning looking for change because they aren't afraid of it, you could put an advertisement online, or as we discussed, you could just talk to people in line outside the Apple store next time Apple releases a new product.

Discover fresh and innovative ways to find talent and you will discover fresh and innovative talent. But once you find them, you need to take them through a Hiring Process that ensures they are a good fit for the mission, the culture, the organization, and the role.

Recall the title of this section: "How Good Is Your Hiring Process?" Do you even know? The uncomfortable truth is that most organizations don't, or they do but it's anemic.

A Culture Advocate is hungry to become excellent at hiring, regardless of her or his role, rank, or level within the organization. A Culture Advocate understands that (while the phrase has become overused) this is a genuine game changer.

Start taking your Hiring Process seriously. I fired a leader once for not doing so, for disrespecting the Hiring Process. It matters that much. It matters so much more than you could ever have imagined when you picked up this book.

The Ultimate Hiring Process

The ultimate Hiring Process is one that is customized for your organization. But you don't need that yet. For now, what you need is a solid plan that is simple enough that it doesn't turn your whole organization upside down and freak everyone out. First things first—it's time to get back to basics.

I always like to start with purpose. It doesn't matter if it is a consulting project, a new product line, a marketing campaign, or, as in this case, an internal process, starting with purpose establishes clarity from the outset.

The purpose of your Hiring Process is to establish a standardized system that increases the chance of hiring the very best employees available for your organization.

Standardization is obviously central to the process. Each candidate should have a very similar experience interviewing with your organization. As time passes and you refine your Hiring Process, current employees will jokingly say, "I'm glad this process wasn't around when I was interviewing; otherwise I probably wouldn't be working here." They are only half joking. And as the process improves, the quality of candidates you attract will improve.

One of the amazing benefits of a really good Hiring Process is the way it builds confidence in everyone involved. When leaders come to me and say, "I would like to hire this person for this role," my favorite question is, "Can she do the role?" If the Hiring Process is solid, the leader can say yes with confidence. They don't need to say anything else. If the Hiring Process is weak, the leader will fumble this question, stammer a bit, and finally say something like, "I think so." My follow-up question is always, "Are you confident this person can do the role, or do you hope she can?"

It really is a horrible feeling to be unsure. It's a bad feeling to hire somebody and have them move their family, have their kids change schools, find new doctors and dentists, and everything else a new role imposes on a family if you aren't really sure the person can succeed in the role. There is actually something reckless and irresponsible about that. But it happens all the time.

Hoping a person can do a role is not good enough. You need to be confident she can do the role. You owe your organization that and you owe the candidate that. You know better than she does if she can succeed in the role. If you don't, then your Hiring Process needs some serious work. A great Hiring Process allows you to develop confidence that you have found the right person for the right role—and that confidence is priceless.

The ultimate Hiring Process serves your organization by finding people who can excel in the role they are hired to perform today and have the potential to add even more value in the future. This is just one of the ways the ultimate Hiring Process plays a significant role in helping to build a Dynamic Culture.

The Hiring Process: Crucial Steps

The worst thing you can do when it comes to the Hiring Process is not have one. Even a bad one is better than none at all. It is one of the very few times in life when that is true. If you do have a Hiring Process, there are some questions that may prove enlightening: Does everyone follow the Hiring Process? Do some kings and queens of the organization circumvent it, frustrating those responsible for ensuring the process is used successfully?

Let's take a look at the crucial steps that increase your organization's chances of finding, hiring, and keeping fabulous team members. But first let's look at the typical Hiring Process by examining the type of thing you find online.

A Hiring Process
1. Post role
2. Review applications
3. Select candidates for interview
4. Test a short list of candidates
5. Select the best candidate for the role
6. Check references
7. Prepare offer letter

Now let's consider some questions that arise anytime you put together a Hiring Process.

- Who decides to post a role?
- How do you know you need to hire someone?
- Is it a new role in response to a new opportunity or growth?
- Or are you backfilling a position because someone has left the organization (voluntarily or involuntarily)?
- If you are backfilling a position, what did you learn from the exit interview that would inform the way you hire for this role now?

You'll notice that we have not even gotten to the first item in the sample Hiring Process yet, and I am holding back. A number of significant steps were missed prior to that first item, and it doesn't just matter that these steps get done, it matters who does them or is consulted about them. These all need to be answered before the role is even posted.

- Who reviews applications?
- What criteria are used for reviewing résumés and applications?
- Who set the criteria?
- Does that person have working knowledge of the role and the work this new hire will be doing every day?
- Are the hiring criteria prioritized? Are some essential and others just nice to have? Who knows the difference?

If we don't select the right people to be interviewed, the process is sunk before the first interview. But let's assume the right people are selected—and that is one massive assumption—another whole batch of problems emerges.

- Who will do the interviewing?
- How many people will interview each candidate?
- If it's more than one (and it definitely should be), will the same people interview each candidate for that role, or will different people interview different candidates?
- What questions will be asked during the interview?
- Will each interviewer ask the same questions, making you all look like you have no idea what you are doing as an organization?
- Will each interviewer know what questions the candidate has already been asked?
- Who has the authority to cut the process short and rule out a candidate in order to avoid wasting other people's time if it becomes clear that a candidate is not a good fit?

Dynamic organizations really think this through. It matters to your success as an organization, and it has a profound impact on creating a Dynamic Culture so that people love coming to work and accomplishing great things together.

Now let's take a look at an outline for a rigorous Hiring Process. Keep in mind this outline is for an eighty-five-page custom Hiring Process document developed and refined over a four-year period for one organization.

A Dynamic Hiring Process
1. Approval received for a new or backfill position
2. HR conducts a Needs Assessment with the Hiring Leader
3. Role Description* and Scorecard are finalized
4. The role is posted
5. Sourcing of candidates begins
6. Hiring Leader screens applications
7. HR conducts phone screen
8. Hiring Leader conducts phone screen
   a. Prior to interview with Hiring Leader, candidate completes the Myers-Briggs assessment
9. On-site interviews
   a. The Career Interview
   b. The Deep Dive Interview
   c. The Culture Interview
10. A Candidate Debrief is conducted
11. Reference Check
12. Conditional Offer is made for the role (contingent on passing background check)

I don't call them job descriptions anymore. Two reasons: People want more than just a job; and organizations don't want their employees to treat their work like just a job. I'd invite you to call them Role Descriptions, and eradicate the word job *from your vocabulary and the vocabulary of your organization.*

Now, resist the temptation to get overwhelmed. If you are a small business, don't even think about a Hiring Process this complex; stick with the basics. Whatever size organization you work in, you may not even know what some of these things are. And that's OK. Just don't lose sight of the main point: You need a Hiring Process, and you need to ensure it is followed with rigor and discipline.

There are also some common mistakes you need to avoid. There is always going to be the temptation to skip steps—don't! You may think, "Calling references is only one piece of this whole process," or "This candidate doesn't need the Cultural Interview; I can already tell he is a great fit for our culture." People make this mistake all the time. We tell ourselves it's just one little piece, but you'd be amazed how often one reference call can illuminate things you heard in the interviews but didn't really hear, and saw but didn't really see. Perhaps you call the reference and discover that the person named was the candidate's colleague, but not the candidate's leader. Find that leader. The exception would be if your candidate doesn't want their current employer to know he or she is looking for a new position with another company.

You have to remember that people are better trained and prepared to interview than ever before. I'm sorry to point out the tragically obvious again, but in many cases potential employees are better prepared for the interviews than organizations are to hire.

If you are going to miss steps, you might as well throw the whole process out, because it will be the step you miss that comes back to get you. Do not trust yourself when it comes to hiring. It will be your downfall. The best attitude is to believe you are bad at hiring. This kind of humility will position you to respect the process appropriately.

Your Hiring Process doesn't need to be complicated, but it needs the basics, it needs to be respected, and it needs to be followed every single time, for every single open position, by every single person in the organization.

The future of your organization is in peril without a Hiring Process.

The Interview Process

How would you feel about marrying someone after the first date? I respect people's choice to do so if they are so inclined, but that seems like a high-risk decision. Now, you are probably wondering why I am even talking about these things. The reason is to provide context, because organizations do this all the time.

Your boss gets a call from a friend who tells him about the son of a friend who is looking for work and would be a perfect fit for your organization. Your boss completely circumvents the Hiring Process and unilaterally decides to hire this person. First-date marriages in the corporate world almost never work. A candidate is invited in for an interview, which is cursory at best, then you throw in a bad muffin, doughnut, or cookie, and suddenly it's: "When can you start?"

Outlined clearly in writing, these scenarios seem ridiculous, until we realize, "Wow, these things actually happen." And they happen far too often. But that doesn't make them any less ridiculous.

Rule No. 1 when it comes to interviewing candidates: Do not rush. You will fail. You will make mistakes. They will cost you. Schedule interviews when you know you will be at your best, when you won't be distracted or in a rush. Interviewing candidates is difficult. Hiring people is incredibly difficult. Give yourself the best possible chance at success.

Rule No. 2: Don't be afraid to get outside the box. People are very good at interviewing today. They are good at putting their best foot forward. This is natural and normal, but the truth is you are trying to get to know people on a deeper level in a compressed period of time. You want to know as much of the good, the bad, and the ugly and dysfunctional as possible. In order to accomplish this, you need to get outside the box and do something unexpected. Knock them off their game a little. Not to be mean or play games, but so that you can get to *real* as quickly as possible.

My favorite way to interview people is to have the candidates interview each other. Narrow down the candidates to six to eight, and then invite them all to visit your organization's HQ or another location on the same day at the same time. Put them all together in a conference room, give them an hour to get to know each other as a group; then give them fifteen minutes with each of the other candidates to interview each other one at a time with this question and instruction as context: If we were hiring two people for this kind of role and you were the first person we hired, who in the room should be the other person we hire and why? If we shouldn't hire a particular candidate, write down the reasons why.

It is amazing what you will learn. It is astounding the things they will tell each other that they won't tell you. By the time you sit down with the candidates, you will already know so much about each of them, and you will have tons of inspiration for unique questions to ask beyond those set out in your Hiring Process. And yes, your Hiring Process should include specific questions, and every candidate should be asked these same questions. You can ask them others, but the core questions don't change. You may also have some personal favorite questions. One of mine is: What are you reading at the moment? I find that what people read gives you a unique insight into their passions and interests, and people who are committed to continuous improvement tend to be readers. The person who says jokingly, "I haven't read a book since high school," is telling you something.

Every Hiring Process should have set questions for each interview. Asking all the candidates these same questions matters. At the end of each interview, I like to give candidates an overall score between 1 and 10 as an easy reference point later.

Let's take a look at a standard Career Interview from the Hiring Process outlined earlier.

The Career Interview
Date:
Position:
Name of Candidate:
Interviewer (Primary):
Interviewer (Secondary):
Note: Prior to the interview, review the candidate's résumé and the Role Description and Scorecard for the role.

———————

Open the interview by explaining to the candidate what they can expect. How long will the interview last? What will be covered? What are your desired outcomes? Then give the candidate a chance to ask any questions about what you have just shared.

Note: This is not the time for general questions the candidate may have, just an opportunity for them to ask any questions they may have about the process for today's interview.

This might sound something like:

"Thanks for coming in today, Melissa. We are excited to explore the possibility of you coming to work with us here at XYZ Corp. During this interview, which we call the Career Interview, we are going to spend sixty to ninety minutes asking you a set of specific questions about your employment history. We will work through your résumé backwards in chronological order. Perhaps we could begin by discussing your role as [role] at [organization]."

Avoid the temptation to jump around out of backward chronological order; and if the candidate tries to do that, refocus them on the proper order.

Interview Questions:

1. What were you hired to do?

   Nudge Questions:

   a. What skills did you need to succeed in this role?

   b. How would you describe your responsibilities?

   c. How did you know if you were doing a good job?

   d. What measurements were used to determine how successfully you were fulfilling the role?

2. What accomplishments were you most proud of in this role?

3. Tell us about some of your challenges and failures in that role.

Nudge Questions:
   a. What was the worst thing you experienced?
   b. Describe for us some of the biggest mistakes you
      made in that role.
   c. What would you do differently if you were starting
      that role today?
   d. What didn't you like doing? What were the least
      enjoyable parts of the job?
   e. Can you name two people whose careers you have
      improved? How?

4. Let's talk about some of the people you worked with
   while you were in that role.
   a. What was your leader's name?
   b. How would you describe him/her to a member of
      your family?
   c. What will your leader say are your greatest strengths
      when we speak with him/her?
   d. In what ways will he/she say you have room to
      improve? Do you agree with him/her?
   e. What will your team members say you were excellent
      at?
   f. How will they say you have opportunities to grow?

5. Why did you leave [organization] and that role? OR: Why
   are you looking to leave [organization] and your role as
   [role]?
   Nudge Questions:
   a. How would joining our organization further your
      career?
   b. When most people leave an organization, they are

usually running away from something and toward something else. In your own situation, what do you think you are running away from and what do you think you are running toward?

6. Does your leader know you are leaving? If he/she does, how did you tell your leader that you were leaving, and what was his/her reaction? If you have not told your leader, how do you think he/she will react?

7. How did (or would) you feel once your colleagues all knew you were leaving?
   Nudge Question:
   a. How did you feel the last time you walked out of [organization]?
   b. What do you fear about leaving your current role?

8. Tell us about the time in your life when you worked the hardest and longest hours to accomplish something.

Note: This interview would obviously need to be adapted if you are hiring a recent graduate or hiring someone for their first professional role.

Post-Interview Huddle Questions:
These questions are used to guide a conversation between all those who interviewed or interacted with a candidate during his or her visit to your organization.

1. Would you be excited to work with this person every day? If so, why?

2. On a scale of 1 to 10, how confident are you that the candidate could do the role?

3. What is it about the candidate's track record that makes you believe he or she could meet *every* outcome on the Scorecard?

4. How do you think this person would respond to feedback?

5. Could you have a direct, tough, straight-to-the-point conversation with this candidate about his or her performance? How would this person respond to the radical candor that is at the heart of our organization's success?

6. What is it about this role that the candidate is most attracted to: the role itself, the mission, or the benefits?

7. If you had to make a recommendation right now about hiring this candidate, and your only options were *definitely yes* and *definitely no*, which would it be?

Develop Your Own Hiring Playbook

Great coaches guard their playbooks with their lives. They are a treasured possession, because they can be the difference between winning and losing.

Whenever there is an economic downturn, I encourage people to take notes about the things they observe and the lessons they learn, and I always remind them that even in a recession more than 10 percent of businesses are having their best year ever.

The economy moves in cycles, and most people don't have a playbook for an economic downturn even if they have experienced several. However, if your organization decides to involve you in the Hiring Process, get a notebook and keep notes. You don't need to take tons and tons of notes about every candidate;

instead, the purpose of your personal hiring playbook is to keep a record of the universal themes and lessons that you observe. I suggest you also have a section for red flags.

What red flags do you look for when you are interviewing people? I love asking leaders and HR professionals this question. You don't have to take all the hard knocks yourself to arrive at wisdom. You don't need to learn every lesson the hard way. Experience is not the only teacher. The wisest people learn from other people's mistakes (and for that very reason they usually have a love of history).

There are red flags that are obvious, such as when someone interviewing for a role to maintain relationships with the most significant donors for a nonprofit organization is socially awkward. But there are a lot of red flags that are much subtler, like not giving specific examples of the work that was involved in a previous role.

Here are some more examples of red flags to be on the lookout for as you interview candidates and work through your Hiring Process. (Not every red flag is a problem for every role. If, for instance, you have a socially awkward accountant who is going to be auditing financials in an out-of-the-way office at your HQ and he is exceptional at his role, then the socially awkward red flag isn't necessarily a deal breaker.)

- Candidates who don't know anything about your organization, and haven't even bothered to spend time on your website getting to know you
- Candidates who deflect, dodge, or seem unable to answer the tough questions
- Candidates incapable of saying anything negative about themselves, or who try to make their negatives look like positives

- Unexplained gaps in someone's résumé or work history
- The absence of longevity in any one role; for example, a candidate who has had seven roles in ten years
- Candidates who do not respect any of their past leaders, and have left one or more roles because of a disagreement with their leader
- Candidates who overemphasize how toxic the culture at their last organization was and are unable to say what efforts they made to improve it
- Candidates who seem resistant to being held accountable for specific deliverables and have never been held accountable in this way before
- Candidates who act unprofessionally: lacking respect for the opportunity; are late for the interview; gossip about past leaders or colleagues; dress inappropriately; or display personal habits that are incongruent with the behavior of a professional
- Candidates who only ask about financial compensation, other employee benefits, and how the culture will serve their personal lifestyle
- Candidates who make demands up front before they will even consider the role
- Candidates who are willing to take a significant pay cut. They usually end up giving less, feeling like you owe them something, and becoming resentful.
- Any candidate who interrupts you. Once, OK, you can give them the benefit of the doubt, depending on the reason for the interruption. More than once and that is a problem, mostly because it is likely to be a symptom of a much bigger problem: not being a good listener.
- Candidates who parrot what they read on your website,

or what someone else shared with them in the screening interview

- Candidates who have no questions
- College graduates who think they are special, behave in a way that is entitled, and are used to being pandered to
- Self-absorbed candidates. These people will struggle to play well with teams.
- Candidates who will try to impress you by telling you proprietary information that is clearly in violation of standard business practices and their previous employment contract. These candidates cannot be trusted to hold any of your proprietary information confidential.
- If the candidate seems too good to be true, he or she probably is. Keep probing. Take extra time or do an additional interview, and make extra reference calls for this type of candidate. You may have found the perfect candidate—and I hope you have—but you may also have found a master of charm, manipulation, and creating a narrative that does not match up to reality.

There is an art to interviewing people who apply to work at your organization, but there is also a science to it. Don't ignore the science—it is the systems and processes that protect you from making hiring mistakes. Hiring mistakes are painful for the individual and the organization. They are costly for an organization in many ways, including financial, lost opportunities, and organizational or team morale.

If I could implement one practice when it comes to hiring, I would not let anybody make a hiring decision until they had fired somebody. This is not possible, but I would do it if I could.

What you can do is put together a mock firing. Tell the person hiring that they have to prepare to fire the person who sits three desks away. Give them a week's notice to get ready and lie awake at night like you do when you have to let someone go.

It is a horrible thing to have to terminate someone's employment. These are the types of things that weigh very heavily on the hearts of leaders of goodwill. I have had to do it my fair share of times throughout my career, because of hiring mistakes I have made and hiring mistakes other people have made. It has always been a heart-wrenching experience for me. The first time I had to let an employee go, I was twenty-four years old and he was more than twice my age.

The people you hire will have a huge impact on your culture. If you want to build a Dynamic Culture, one of the best places to start is with recruiting, hiring, and onboarding. Few things are more impactful and more neglected at the same time than hiring.

Culture Advocates Are Talent Fanatics

There is something immensely satisfying about finding a really special person for your organization, whether it is a janitor or a director of finance. A janitor with a great attitude can have a huge impact on a culture; so can one with a horrible attitude.

One thing I have noticed about Culture Advocates is that they are also talent fanatics. Wherever they go, they are always looking for great people to join their organization. If they have a great service experience at a car dealership or at a restaurant, they ask themselves, "Is there a place for this person at work?" Most of the time there isn't at that moment, but they file that person away in their mind or make a note in their playbook for future reference.

It is time for every person in your organization to become

a talent fanatic. These may seem like just words on a page, an emphatic call to action, but it is so much more than that. The stakes are high, just from the perspective of our daily experience of work, and it is very important that we make ourselves aware of how much this matters and all that is at stake.

Better hiring decisions lead to more successful organizations and more Dynamic Cultures. The better you hire, the less time your leaders need to spend managing or micromanaging, and the more time they spend coaching people to the next level. Great hires are more self-driven and better at self-management than the average employee. This frees up leaders to spend more time on what matters most: growing their people and growing the business. Great leaders are hungry for time to drive real improvement (rather than cosmetic improvement) by coaching their people instead of just issuing objectives.

Better hiring decisions lead to less drama at work—and aren't we all sick of drama at work?

Better hiring decisions prevent the best team members from having to redo the work of substandard employees, freeing up your best people to do even more great work. Give your best people some white space on their calendars and prepare to be amazed by what they do with it.

Better hiring decisions increase compensation and employee benefits in the future.

The Stakes Are High

There is so much more at stake than most people realize. Every hiring decision reaches into every corner of the organization and influences every aspect of the culture.

But let's get brutally honest with each other for a moment.

Once a month the US Department of Labor announces unemployment numbers. These numbers fluctuate every month and have varied radically at different times. During World War I the unemployment rate was 1 percent, during the Great Depression it was 25 percent, and it was 10.8 percent and 10 percent during the Recessions of 1982 and 2009, respectively. The unemployment rate as I am writing this chapter is 4.1 percent. But these numbers only include adults who are actively seeking work, and we all know there are plenty who are not.

The reality is that beyond the 4.1 percent who are unemployed, there are probably at least 10 percent who are unemployable. Not unemployed, unemployable. I am not speaking of those who are disabled and other legitimate exemptions from the unemployment calculations. I am speaking of people who simply do not want to work because they would rather leech off their family, friends, and society in general.

There is one more factor, lurking just below the surface of mainstream society, that we all know is there but almost never talk about. As people's lives become more dysfunctional, the number of people who will exit the workforce will increase dramatically.

The main driver and perhaps the biggest social issue of the next fifty years will be addiction. It is impossible to calculate the cost of addiction to business and the economy as a whole today, but whatever that number is, it is going to escalate beyond belief in the next twenty years. We have removed and rejected so much of what held the foundation of society together that the number of individual lives, families, and communities that are crumbling and will crumble under the destructive weight of addiction will be astonishing. This one factor may double the number of people who are simply unemployable in the next twenty years. That is, they cannot be relied upon to show up to work on time on a regular basis and execute even the most basic tasks.

Add to that the fact that birth rates are hitting all-time lows, as well as the great unspoken tragedy of our culture, and now you have the makings of a perfect storm. What is the great unspoken tragedy of our culture? For all the rhetoric about our children being our future, our education system is an epic failure. High schools and colleges are churning out graduates who know more and more about less and less, and along the way we are completely failing to give them the most basic life skills.

Let's consider just one example: personal finances. The number of young adults with absolutely no understanding of personal finances is appalling. We use money every day. In the life-skills department, too many people know far too little about how to earn, save, spend, and give money. And this is equivalent to breathing. I don't know how we think our young people are going to learn to breathe financially if we don't teach them.

All these factors are leading us toward possibly the most significant (and difficult to solve) problems the corporate world has ever faced. Make no mistake, we are about to witness the largest shortage of talent ever. This will lead to an unprecedented war for talent. The phrase is not new to the corporate vocabulary, but what we have seen so far (even in the tech industry) have been mere skirmishes compared to the outright war that is coming. Corporations may start their own high schools and colleges to properly prepare a workforce, and I also think corporate warfare or corporate terrorism should not be ruled out as a possibility in the near future.

The stakes when it comes to hiring are very high. To forget that is to fumble the ball on culture in the first play of the game. There is a lot to learn and a lot to know about hiring.

The One Immutable Law of Hiring

This is the one immutable law when it comes to hiring: If it is not a definite yes, it's a definite no.

There is no such thing as good enough when it comes to hiring. You will be sorry if you break this law—every single time—because it invites mediocrity into your organization. People will be putting pressure on you to hire someone you know is a bad fit for the role, for the culture, or both. "Just get me a warm body." You will actually hear things this stupid. Don't do it.

This is the shortest section of the book. I intentionally kept it very short so that it would be impossible to miss the message.

If it is not a definite yes, it's a definite no. This is the one immutable law when it comes to hiring. Write it on the wall for everyone to see. Use it as a mantra when speaking to everyone and anyone involved in the Hiring Process. Allow this single idea to guide you when you are hiring and you will save many people inside and outside the organization a lot of pain and suffering. How do you think a ten-year-old child feels the day his mother or father comes home and has been fired? These are the things we need to consider before we hire recklessly, just hoping it works out.

If it is not a definite yes, it's a definite no. It's a pretty good maxim, not just for hiring, but for life too.

One Patient Person in an Impatient World

We spoke earlier about how the average person's life is becoming more dysfunctional. This dysfunction can largely be linked to the fact that society is doing everything within its power to cast patience and discipline out of our lives. The more impatient and undisciplined we become, the less capable we become of excellence in any aspect of life, and hiring requires the patience of Job and the discipline of an elite athlete.

If you want to get really good at hiring, you will need the patience to wait for the right candidate, the willingness to go out and find the right candidate, and the discipline to say no to candidates who are not a good fit for the role or culture.

Do not rush. Become the most patient person you know. Don't act out of desperation. Always hire from a position of strength, never from a place of weakness (even if you are desperate and weak). Stay mindful of how you felt the last time you had to let someone go.

Over a ten-year period, 80 percent of money managers underperform the S&P 500 Index, because we have a bias as human beings toward action. We have a bias toward doing something versus not doing something. Sometimes there are long periods when the best thing for a money manager to do is nothing.

Sometimes the hardest thing to do is to do nothing. The discipline not to do anything, not to act, not to hire when you know a candidate cannot deliver on the Role Description and the Scorecard is not easy. There are very few organizations, recruiters, and Hiring Leaders who have that very specific discipline, but it can be the difference between extraordinary success and second-rate mediocrity. Depending on the size, age, growth rate, and hiring rate of your organization, this one factor could be the difference between building a Dynamic Culture where people love coming to work to accomplish great things together and a culture where people are deeply unhappy.

The people you hire and the way you recruit and hire new employees sends a message to everyone in your organization.

Use that to your advantage. Hire in a way that sends a message, "This place is different." You can hire in a way that says, "This is a place where lazy people can come and hide, work like a minimalist by doing the very least to get by, and never be called to task." Or you can hire in a way that sends the message, "This is a Dynamic Culture where people are hungry for best practices and continuous improvement, a place where we strive to be the very best at what we do by being committed, coachable, and aware."

As people go through the interview process, they should very quickly get the sense that your organization is different, that it values rigor and excellence. In fact, you should tell them up front once they get beyond the screening interview that this process is going to different. The process has to be long enough to discover if a candidate is the right person for the role and the culture, and once you get your culture to a great place, people should truly want to work there.

The discipline of hiring and firing is essential to the health, culture, and success of the organization. It is a discipline that requires tremendous patience and intentionality, one that will pay dividends to your culture every single day if it is embraced.

How Would You Feel?

There is probably someone on your team who needs to go. When you read that line, if you are a leader, you have probably already identified that person in your mind. It took a split second. If you are a leader, let me ask you this question: What are you waiting for and why are you dragging your feet?

You know it, the employee knows it, and your team knows it, but you are dragging your feet. That is hurting your brand as a leader, because your team thinks you are either an idiot because you haven't recognized the reality, or worse, that you are aware and are ignoring or tolerating it. When we tolerate mediocrity, we discourage excellence.

There are certain questions that bring great clarity to situations like these in which we tend to act on emotion. The main emotion that blocks our good judgment in firing is cowardice. In the grips of cowardice, it is so easy to set aside what is best for the culture, the other employees, the customers, and the organization. Mediocrity and cowardice are cousins.

Consider these two questions:

1. If you knew when you interviewed that person what you know today, would you have hired that person?
2. How would you feel if that person came in first thing tomorrow and told you he or she was leaving for another role? Relieved? That's how most team leaders answer the question.

Every leader makes hiring mistakes. Ask a few leaders and you will hear some shocking stories. It does happen. The question is what we do once we realize it.

My advice: If you make a mistake, do yourself, the mission, and the person you hired a favor and act quickly. Take action, as soon as possible. If you think you can coach that person up to where you need him to be, great. Do it. Put together a thirty-day plan. Explain clearly that he is not meeting your expectations and the requirements of the role, and give him thirty days to raise his performance. If he doesn't, let him go. He will probably thank you for it someday. I cannot tell you how many people I have let go who have come back to me a year or two later and thanked me for doing so, because it forced them to really think about what they could be great at and enjoy.

We hire too quickly and fire too slowly. A great Hiring Process should reverse these realities. Hire slowly and fire quickly. Don't be afraid to let someone go when that is what the situation requires. Mission Is King. Never lose sight of that. Indecisiveness when action is clearly needed weakens the whole organization.

Organizations with Dynamic Cultures are good at hiring and good at firing employees. In order to get good at both hiring and firing, we all need to take to heart the advice I once heard a young human resources team member give the leadership team at the organization where he works: "You need to get comfortable being uncomfortable."

As soon as he said it, I remember thinking to myself, "Wow! That is really good." It's brilliant, actually. It perfectly captures why we don't do what is best for the mission in so many situations—because we don't like being uncomfortable.

When you are interviewing someone and you ask a question and they don't answer, the temptation is to step in and talk more. Don't. I know, that silence can be uncomfortable. Get comfortable being uncomfortable.

It is incredibly uncomfortable when you realize you have made a hiring mistake and you need to let someone go. If you weren't uncomfortable, you would be lacking empathy and your emotional intelligence would probably be fairly limited. You need to get comfortable being uncomfortable.

Hiring is not for the faint of heart. Be decisive or you will breed mediocrity, and sooner or later mediocrity leads to the death of an organization. Hiring and firing is about mission, clarity, culture, and decisiveness. It is at the heart of a Dynamic Culture. Sooner or later an organization rises or falls based on its ability to hire and retain the right people.

A Great Hiring Process Is Essential to a Dynamic Culture

The right people are the foundation of any great organization. Everything great in history has been built by people who believed that the future could be bigger than the past. Finding and growing great people is central to creating a Dynamic Culture.

At the core of these efforts to build dynamic teams that execute world-class projects is a Hiring Process that attracts and identifies the very best person for each role in your organization. If you don't have a Hiring Process, you need one as soon as possible. Start with something simple. If you do have one, how good is it? Does it need revising, updating, improving? Each year FLOYD helps many organizations develop or update their Hiring Process. We would be honored to help you in this way.

This one area can be a cultural game changer. Decide right now to get really good at finding, hiring, and developing talent. Wherever you are in the organization, decide right now to become very familiar with the Hiring Process and participate in it fully according to your role. Never lose sight of what is at stake when it comes to hiring: everything. Everything else flows from hiring. Get it right and a lot of other great things just seem to fall into place.

Culture matters, and hiring really matters when it comes to building a Dynamic Culture. So, remember what we have learned.

- Most organizations are bad at hiring. Get good at hiring and it becomes a massive competitive advantage.
- You cannot build a great culture without getting good at hiring, and you cannot get good at hiring without a great Hiring Process.
- The ultimate Hiring Process takes time to develop, and it is always evolving based on the needs of the organization.

- As soon as a candidate begins to participate in the interview process with your organization, it should be clear that *this place is different* in a really good way. Your interview process should be so good that people are begging you to work at your organization.
- When it comes to hiring, there is one immutable law: If it is not a definite yes, it's a definite no. Honor your current employees, honor your mission, and honor your organization by never sidestepping this law.
- Hiring mistakes are very costly both for the organization and individually. It is costly for the organization in terms of profitability and disruption. Individually, a hiring mistake ends up causing a lot of pain and suffering for the employee, his or her family, and the people who work with and lead that person.
- People will always want to ignore, skip, or circumvent part or all of the Hiring Process. *Don't let them.* As a leader, make it clear that you support the Hiring Process 100 percent, and come down hard on people who don't.

Culture Advocates are constantly on the lookout for great talent. If they are involved directly in the Hiring Process, they are hiring maniacs, meaning they have a Hiring Process and they stick to it, always.

Hiring is incredibly difficult. As a consultant, I have developed my own playbook, filled with ideas and maxims. I will share two maxims from my playbook that are applicable to almost every aspect of life and business. The first: Never automatically accept the premise of the question. The second: Question the assumptions. When it comes to hiring, the premise and the assumption that most organizations accept is that the people they need and want to hire will apply for the role. Nothing could be further from the truth. The people you really want to hire probably already have a really good role.

The final secret to becoming great at hiring the right person for every single role is that there is no secret. People and organizations that are really good at hiring don't have a superpower; they simply have a process and follow it. They allow the process to work for them. They never think of the process as inconvenient, and they don't allow themselves to become slaves to it. They see the Hiring Process as a very valuable servant who helps them find the right people and protects them from hiring the wrong people, so that the organization can best accomplish its mission.

I cannot stress enough the importance of having a great Hiring Process. It is critical, not optional. If you want to build a Dynamic Culture, get really serious about hiring, and develop a dynamic Hiring Process.

Sometimes we lose sight of the fact that one of the most rewarding aspects of business is gathering together a group of people to accomplish something, nurturing them, giving them the tools and opportunities they need to succeed, coaching and encouraging them, and celebrating with them when they accomplish the great things you always knew they could. But it all starts with gathering the right group of people.

The Fourth Principle:
HIRE WITH RIGOROUS DISCIPLINE

6

your brand

Brand You Inc.

Let's think back to our discussion at the beginning of chapter two about products and brands that surprise and delight. Everything that we have discussed about products, services, experiences, and culture also applies directly to you. Your work is a product. It is a service. Your presence in the workplace is an experience for other people. You have a brand. Does your brand surprise and delight? Does your work surprise and delight?

Your internal customers are your team leader, other corporate leaders, your colleagues, and especially any person, team, or department you supply a specific work product to. Your external customers are the end users of the product or service that your organization produces and sells. Depending on what your role is, you may never meet your external customer, but you are surrounded by your internal customers every day.

It is also important to remember that you have a brand. What's your brand? If I sat your internal customers down in a focus group setting and asked them questions about you, your work, and your participation as a team member in the organization, what would they tell me? What would be the common themes? What brand would we fall upon?

Some people are branded as the first person to leave every day. That's their brand. They might not even know it, but that is the thing that others think about in relation to them. Other people have a brand for always making it happen. Anyone who has ever had a personal assistant knows how important this quality is, because once you pass something off to your assistant, you want to never have to think about it again. When you first start working with someone, you ask him to circle back with you and let you know that something has been done. But if that person is really good at his role, over time you just trust that if you passed it over to him, he has either taken care of it or will come back to you.

So yes, products and organizations have brands, but so do people.

We can surprise and delight our boss, the people we lead, other team members, customers, and even the whole marketplace. Everyone has a part to play in an organization's culture; it is not solely the burden and responsibility of the CEO.

You have the power to surprise and delight. The question is, are you using it? There are a thousand ways to surprise and delight and build your personal brand each day. Help someone else meet a deadline. Go the extra mile for a customer—internal or external. Get lunch for someone who is a little more under the gun than you today. Express your appreciation to someone who partnered with you on a project. Sure, it was their responsibility, but appreciation and recognition are among the most valuable and underused currencies on the planet. Recognize someone authentically in front of their spouse, children, or parents and you have struck gold. Encourage someone who seems to be struggling. Take a few minutes to ask someone how they are doing—not surface stuff; take a real interest in a peer, colleague, or direct report as a human being completely independent of the organization's goals and the work you do together. Offer to help. Offer to coach or mentor someone for a specific period of time or around a specific skill. Just have a good attitude. Do a bit more. Do something that needs doing even though nobody asked you to do it.

Interestingly, developing a great culture is actually a very sensible thing to do from a self-interest perspective. By adopting a surprise-and-delight attitude in everything you do at work, you are advancing your brand and career. Developing a personal brand of surprise and delight is in your best interest and an extremely clever way to ensure your place in the organization as someone who adds incredible and indispensable value.

What's your brand?

Amazed!

As a business consultant, I find myself asking people certain questions all the time. One of those questions is: What do you do here? I'm amazed how many employees cannot answer this question in a clear and concise way.

Recall the story about the bricklayers and the Notre-Dame Cathedral. I heard a very similar story about when JFK was president and visiting a NASA facility. During the visit, he unexpectedly met a Culture Advocate. The man was mopping a hallway. That particular hallway had not been an intended part of the president's tour, but he saw a restroom and excused himself from the formal tour to use it.

Seeing the man mopping the floor, the president introduced himself and spoke briefly with the janitor, who beamed with pride at the unexpected opportunity. Noticing this, the president asked him, "Do you enjoy your work here?"

"Oh, yes, Mr. President. It is an honor," the janitor replied.

"Most janitors probably don't feel that way, I suspect," the president proposed.

"Well, Mr. President, I'm older than you, and it seems to me that more and more people just want to be served and don't want to do any serving. But my father taught me that we are all here to serve one another, and we get our dignity and honor by serving."

"What else do you do here?" President Kennedy asked.

The janitor smiled. "I only do one thing here."

"You mop floors all day?" the president inquired.

"Nope," the janitor replied, smiling again. "People see me mopping floors, emptying trash cans, cleaning windows, but in my mind, I am working to put a man on the moon."

The president used the restroom and left. But as he got about ten steps away from the janitor, he turned back to him and said, "Do you think we can do it?"

"Yes sir, Mr. President, I can already see Neil—I mean, Mr. Armstrong—walking on the moon in my mind's eye." President Kennedy turned around, looked down, and smiled as he walked down the hallway to rejoin the dignitaries.

When someone asks you, "What do you do here?" there are only two answers. Everyone should have both at the ready, and should have the awareness to know which is more appropriate.

1. The Aspirational Answer

We should all be able to answer the question like the bricklayer and janitor: "We are building the finest cathedral the world has ever seen." "I am working to put a man on the moon."

For a few years I had a voice mail that said, "Hi, this is Matthew. I'm busy helping someone else fulfill their dream right now, but leave me a message and I'll call you back." It's amazing how many conversations that voice mail triggered, conversations that otherwise probably would never have happened.

The world is full of ordinary, and it doesn't need any more. The aspirational answer connects what we do each day with the larger mission of the team or organization.

2. The Practical Answer

The second answer is more practical. It is disturbing to me how many people cannot clearly and concisely describe their role within an organization. I overheard one of my executive assistants a few weeks ago speaking with a visitor. "So, what do you do here?" the visitor asked.

"I am Mr. Kelly's executive assistant," she replied.

"OK, but what does that mean day-to-day? What is it that you actually do?" the guest pressed her.

"My role is to do anything that will make Mr. Kelly's role and life easier, so he can focus on doing the things that only he can do. Sometimes that means managing his schedule and sometimes it's just making sure he has something to eat for lunch."

The visitor wasn't finished. "But tell me truthfully, what's the hardest part of your role?"

"Saying no gracefully," my assistant replied. "I spend a lot of time saying no to people."

What do you do here? Get clear about that. Why? Lots of reasons, least of which is in case someone asks you. When you can answer the question, you will perform your role at a much higher level. If you don't like the answer to the question, you probably don't like your role, and you should do something about that because life is short. There are many people who woke up this morning who won't go to bed tonight, and many who will go to bed tonight but not wake up tomorrow morning.

What do you do here? If you don't have a compelling answer to the question, it makes me wonder if you should have a role here at all.

The Most Powerful and Neglected Tool in Business

If you cannot put together a decent Role Description for a position, as we discussed earlier, you have no business hiring someone for that role. You may need someone to do that role, but they won't do it well without a focused description.

My colleagues know if they want to add a new position not to come anywhere near me without a Role Description and a Scorecard. (We will talk about Scorecards shortly.) The reality is a well-considered Role Description increases your chances of hiring the right candidate by 50 percent. A great Scorecard increases your chances of hiring the right candidate by another 20 percent. These things really matter, so much more than the vast majority of people in the corporate world understand. I'm begging you to take them seriously.

If your organization already has a way of developing Role Descriptions, great—review it with everything you have learned in these pages in mind. It may be good, it may need tweaking, it may need new life breathed into it, or it may need a complete overhaul. If it needs the latter, do it—you will be so glad you did. You need a phenomenal Role Description template.

Most organizations don't even have a good template, let alone a phenomenal one. That would be considered a complete waste of time by the majority of people in business—which is why corporate waste and mediocrity are so widespread.

What are your chances of hitting a target if I don't tell you what the target is? Right. Next to zero. But we do it to people all the time. A poorly considered and badly written Role Description is a form of corporate violence against employees because it sets them up for failure. It is also a waste of resources, destroys efficiency, and robs people of the joy that comes from doing good work.

Leaders: Do you have a copy of the Role Descriptions for every person who reports to you? Do you have a copy of your own Role Description?

Employees: Do you have a copy of your own Role Description?

I think you can see where we are heading, and it is along the big fat road that leads to the big fat land of mediocrity. The land of mediocrity is getting more crowded every day—full of lazy procrastinators with no direction, who are clueless about what their actual role entails.

In every situation like this there is someone worth envying in a healthy way. In this particular situation, I envy professional athletes. They always know how they are doing—all they have to do is look at the scoreboard; as soon as they walk off the field they are given a bunch of statistics that tell them how they did;

their games and practice sessions are filmed; and their position coach breaks down every play, pointing out nuances to build skills that improve both individual and team performance. That kind of clarity is an incredible gift to give an employee.

That's why a Role Description is not enough. You should have a Scorecard for every employee—before you begin the interview process. It outlines how you are going to measure success, what the key performance indicators will be for this particular role. So, as you are interviewing candidates, you can delve into their past experience to see if they will be able to live up to the Scorecard.

The best indicator of future performance is past performance. If a candidate has not done something in the past that you want them to accomplish in this new role, what makes you think they will be able to deliver? That is called hope, my friend, and hope is a beautiful thing, but it's often misplaced. Hope has no place in the Hiring Process.

You need a Role Description and a Scorecard for every person in your organization. These need to be updated regularly; they should be living, breathing documents. People should have a copy of their own with them at every significant meeting. Every leader should have a copy of the Role Description and Scorecard for every person he or she leads.

The reasons for this are many, but let's quickly list the big ones. Nobody can perform their role if they don't know what the role is. Nobody can achieve excellence if they don't know how it is being measured. You cannot effectively lead people if you don't know what their deliverables are. People deserve to know where they stand and how they are doing.

How will you and, more important, the person doing the role know if he or she is excelling without a clear Role Description and Scorecard? I think we both know the answer: You won't.

A few years ago, FLOYD was invited into an organization to work with their sales team. The organization was young but massively ambitious. They were doing $3 million in sales with a goal of $100 million within ten years. They had twenty-seven salespeople but four guys were producing more than $2 million of the sales. Two of my FLOYD colleagues and I spent four hours with these four salespeople, and it was awesome. For starters, they were annoyed that we had taken them away from their work. It was immediately obvious why they were successful: They were dripping with commitment, a desire to succeed, and a healthy competitiveness.

After talking to the four sales guys, we provided the owners with a list of five qualities and asked them to make copies for the other twenty-three salespeople. We wrote the name of each employee at the top of each sheet, and then we walked through the five qualities with each, asking which of them he or she had. Then we ranked every person on the sales team according to how many of the qualities they had from the list of five. We then asked for a list of the previous month's sales results from best to worst. With the exception of only one person, the lists were identical.

"How did you do that?" one of the owners asked me.

"It doesn't matter," I said. "The point is we did it, and what we now know will take your business to $100 million in annual sales."

"How?"

"What do your top four salespeople have in common other than the five qualities?" I asked the two owners. They didn't know, and they were smart enough not to pretend that they did or fruitlessly guess.

"They were all college athletes. They hate losing. They know how to win. They have been trained to win. You didn't have to train them to win because they already had it in their blood."

"So, what should we do now?"

"Your next five highest performers were also college athletes. They can stay for ninety days with very clear daily, weekly, and monthly goals."

"What about the rest?"

"Gone. Today. It is stupid and immoral to hire someone for a role they have no chance succeeding at."

"Then what?"

"Who does the hiring around here?"

The owners looked at each other and replied, "We do."

"Good. For the next six months you only hire former college athletes, who have at least three of the five qualities on the list."

"What else?"

One side of their office space was all windows and the other side was a wall. "Get rid of all these offices and cubicles; open up this space. On that wall, I want to see a huge scoreboard. Every person on the sales team needs to know in real time how they are doing: for the day, week, month, quarter, year, and lifetime results. They also need to see how their teammates are doing."

They did everything we recommended. In fact, they might be the only client that has ever done everything we suggested. Remember their goal: $100 million in ten years. They did it. But they did it in three years, nine months, and twenty-seven days.

And the culture: competitive, committed, and fun. But the leaders had great values. With the wrong leaders, this could have been a complete disaster. As a leader, you can create either healthy competition or very unhealthy competition. But that is not the main point of the story.

People deserve to know where they stand. They deserve to know how they are doing. That's the main point of the story. People also deserve a chance to win, so they need to know what winning looks like, and when they do win, they deserve to be celebrated.

Originally, I called this chapter "Job Descriptions Matter," but I knew if I called it that, many people wouldn't read it, so I had to change it. As the actual title says, Role Descriptions and Scorecards truly are the most powerful and neglected tools in business. I hope you will start calling them Role Descriptions, but regardless of what you call them, just get really clear that they matter.

Take this seriously. Your culture needs it. Most businesses and most leaders look at creating Role Descriptions as just another box that needs to be checked in order to move on. Most people only ever look at the Role Description when they are applying for a position, and never look at it again, even if they get the role. *Stop.* All this must come to an end if you want to build a Dynamic Culture.

Spend time developing usable Role Descriptions and Scorecards for every person in the organization, and review and refine them at least once a year. Refer to them in the review process. Use them to coach people to constantly improve, and use them to make your expectations abundantly clear. People are not mind readers. They need to know what their role is and what your expectations are.

Role Descriptions are a system, and a very powerful, neglected one at that. Systems drive behavior. Like so much of what we have talked about in this book, you are already doing these things; it is a matter of engaging them in a new way.

Don't get overwhelmed. It doesn't have to be this week or this month, but build this into your Strategic Plan. Respond, don't react. But for any new roles, do it right from the start. Here's how:

a. Develop a template for a Role Description and Scorecard.
b. Test the template across a variety of roles and departments.
c. Write your own Role Description and Scorecard.
d. Distribute the template and ask everyone in the organization to write a first draft of their own Role Description and Scorecard.

Warning: In this chapter, we have talked a lot about setting people up to win. The easiest way to cause even the most talented team member to fail is to give him or her more responsibility than authority. Without sufficient authority to carry out what we are responsible for, even the best are doomed to fail. This usually happens when we want to transition someone into a new role; we give them certain responsibilities and make them accountable for certain results, but we fail to give them the authority to fulfill their commission. Be careful you don't fall into that trap.

A Role Description is a fabulous tool to lead people to succeed. Add in a well-crafted Scorecard and your leaders will be maximizing the potential of their people and teams better than ever before.

These are living, breathing documents; it's important not to forget that. Most people are capable of doing more than we ask and expect them to, and not only are they capable, but they want to do more. Ask them to update their Role Descriptions and many will surprise and delight you.

What could be more mundane than Role Descriptions, right? Wrong. Role Descriptions are powerful tools. Take them seriously and you will be amazed.

What's Your Personal Brand?

Everybody has a brand. Some people's brand is "He is always late"; other people's brands are "She is always so helpful" or "She is always the first to leave." "He is such a hard worker." "She is so committed." The list goes on. Everybody has a personal brand—what do you want yours to be?

Some people overcommit and under-deliver; as a result, their brand becomes unreliable. Some people crush whatever project you give them. That becomes their brand. And every team has that person who wants the ball in those last seconds when it matters most, when one shot is the difference between winning and losing—the person who always comes through when it really matters. That's his personal brand.

Most people's personal brand is developed by default. They didn't set out to create that brand; it just happened. What happens to organizations that just let their brand happen? Right, they probably go out of business.

Organizations spend billions of dollars creating and perpetuating their brand. The least you can do is be intentional about it. What do you want your brand to be? Define it. Then after a year, ask the people you work with to write down anonymously what they think your brand is in the workplace. You'll need thick skin. Great brands have thick skin. Use what you learn from the feedback to hone your brand the following year.

Where should you start? That's up to you, but if you are stuck, start with the big three: Committed, coachable, and aware. If that became your brand, wow, that would be amazing!

If you are committed, coachable, and aware, you will succeed. It is a recipe for success at anything, personally and professionally. Get really, really good at these three things, even if your organization doesn't embrace them. These are the three best things you can do for both your career and your life. Imagine a marriage in which both partners are committed, coachable, and aware. Imagine parents who are committed, coachable, and aware. Imagine being committed, coachable, and aware in the area of personal finance or health and well-being.

The point is, whether we have ever thought about it or not, everyone has a brand, and your brand starts on day one. So, whether today is your first day at an organization or you have been there for ten years, make today day one. When a new president takes office, a lot of attention is paid to what he or she will accomplish in the first one hundred days. If today is your new day one, what are you going to accomplish in your first one hundred days? Take this seriously and a hundred days from now people will be saying, "Wow, she has really stepped it up!"

Whatever you want your brand to be, write it down, read it daily, and do at least one thing every day to demonstrate that brand. Great brands are always before us. I have often wondered what would happen if Coke stopped advertising for a year. They would save billions, but would people drink less Coke after one year? Who knows? Two years? Risky. Five years? I am certain their brand and sales would take a hit. Keep your brand in front of people every day.

There are two things that I am looking to create in everything I do. The first is indisputable value. The organization we talked about in the previous section, we never sent them a bill. The owners asked me what they owed us at the end of the day. I said to them, "Let's do this: We are not going to send you an invoice. Today is the seventh of April—one year from now, send us a check for what you think our services were worth."

The following year on April 7 I received a FedEx envelope with a check for twenty-five times what we would have billed them. Not only that—every year for the next seven years (until they sold the business), they sent us a check on April 7. My FLOYD colleagues and I had created indisputable value for them, and they were classy enough to recognize it.

I've done that a handful of times in my career. It's a mixed bag, but it tells you a lot about the character of the people you serve. My team transformed the business of a woman whose COO had left three years earlier and the business was tanking. We made the same deal with her. One year later she sent me a check for less than one-tenth of what we would have billed her just for our time. Some people are givers and some people are takers, and that's life.

We love creating indisputable value. It's beyond surprise and delight.

Go to work each morning looking to create indisputable value and I can promise you a rich and rewarding career and life. Creating indisputable value is its own reward. It doesn't matter if anyone notices, compliments you for it, or even pays you for it. The best things in life are their own reward. They don't need to be acknowledged by anybody else. Generosity is its own reward. Doing great work is its own reward. Raising children is its own reward. Nobody else even needs to know about things that are their own reward. We can just hold them in our hearts and treasure them. That's what makes things such as random acts of kindness or unexpected acts of love cause our hearts and souls to dance for joy.

Indisputable value is hard to find, but not that hard to create. How do you know when you are creating indisputable value at work? You become indispensable, which is no joke. Would your leader be miserable if you said you were leaving?

The Culture Advocate isn't looking for a pat on the back or an award; fulfilling this role is its own reward. It makes each day better, lighter, and more purposeful, and injects your life with fun and laughter. Culture Advocates create indisputable value.

The other thing I love is searching for the unique. We live in a world of typical. If you drive down most streets, the houses are pretty typical, but occasionally you will be struck by one that is unique. There could be a thousand things that make it unique, but that is the house that everyone looks at when they drive down that street. It's eye-catching.

Walk into a bar and what do you find? A whole bunch of guys who are typical and a whole bunch of women who are typical. Two minutes of conversation reveals just how typical they are. This is the frustration of the soulful single person.

Set out to be unique. Make it part of your personal brand. Don't be like everyone else. Find something deep within yourself that is truly you and cling to it. We spend so much of our lives trying to be and become everything that everyone wants us to be and become. Start by unbecoming all that, then search for what is truly unique within yourself, and give that to the world in small portions each day. Decide to be unique in a world of typical.

Is this still a business book? Yes, that's how it will be classified. But there is an awful lot of crossover between business and life within these pages. Lots of lessons for work and home, I hope. And let's never lose sight of the reality that people don't exist for businesses; businesses exist for people. The future of any great organization depends upon finding and nurturing enough unique talent to carry it into the unknown future.

Whatever we do for work, we should do it in a professional manner. Most people expect to be treated like professionals, but relatively few behave like professionals. I often hear people say, "If you want to be treated like a professional, act like one." I disagree. Don't *act like* one—*be* one. Everything a professional does has a touch of class that sets her apart. I have seen it in personal assistants and I have seen it in CEOs, and in every other role under the sun. I have seen fruit pickers who were more professional than leaders of whole brands within Fortune 500 organizations.

Be a professional. Whatever it is you choose to do, even if it's just something you decide to do while you are discerning what you really want to do, approach it as a professional. Approaching anything as a professional will help you develop business skills and life skills that are portable—skills that are uniquely yours to own and cherish, that you can take wherever you go in life.

Committed, coachable, aware, surprise and delight, indisputable value, unique, and last but not least, professional. Take these, leave these; it doesn't matter to me. But take your personal brand seriously.

The Expectations Gap

The expectations gap is based on the very simple reality that human beings have expectations about everything and everyone. The number one enemy of any brand—your organization's brand and your personal brand—is the expectations gap. It is the Bermuda Triangle of life and business. Failure to understand this single concept has killed more brands, relationships, products, teams, careers, and businesses than any other concept.

If you advertise a brand of toothpaste with the promise that it will whiten teeth and it doesn't do that, you create an expectations gap.

If you tell your spouse you will be home from work tonight at six thirty and you are late, you create an expectations gap, and with every minute after 6:31 that you are not home, the gap widens.

If you promise your direct reports that you will help them map out career paths this year and you don't make the time to do it, you create an expectations gap.

If you tell a customer you will finish a project by June but don't finish until September, you have created an expectations gap.

If you tell your daughter you will take her to the zoo on Saturday and you don't—whether your daughter is five or twenty-five years old—you create an expectations gap.

What is an expectations gap? *The space between what people expect to happen and what actually happens.* People have expectations about everything and everyone. Everyone in your life has expectations of you, and every customer your organization serves has expectations. The problem is *something has to fill the gap.* One of five things, or some combination of those five things, always fill expectations gaps: disappointment, resentment, anger, frustration, and loss of trust.

Now, I don't know about you, but I don't want anyone feeling these five things about me, or about my team, or about any of the products and services offered by the various businesses and organizations I own or am involved with. And I don't know a single person who does. This is a 100 percent issue. The expectations gap is to be avoided at *almost* any cost.

Managing Expectations

It is important to point out, however, that avoiding the expectations gap doesn't mean you need to give everyone what they want all the time and become a doormat personally or professionally.

There will be many situations, both personal and professional, in which you encounter people who have unreasonable expectations. For example, if you are leading a project and the customer starts expressing expectations that are beyond the scope of the contract, those expectations need to be managed. You cannot simply ignore unrealistic expectations; you must manage them. If the customer insists on accommodations beyond the scope of the contract, then you need to renegotiate the contract.

We all have unrealistic expectations about something—probably many things. In our personal lives, we are constantly negotiating and compromising around reasonable and unreasonable expectations. These conversations take place between husband and wife, parents and children, and, as parents get older, between children and parents. The key to managing expectations is communication. When communication breaks down, everything breaks down.

Leading with Clear Expectations

There are two main reasons things don't get done in any organization. No. 1: Leaders don't create clear, mutually agreed-upon, written expectations. No. 2: Even if No. 1 does get done, leaders and team members don't hold each other accountable for those clearly defined written expectations.

If you are a leader, one of your central roles is to make your expectations clear for each of the people you lead. They cannot read your mind. If you don't make your expectations clear, they are unlikely to be met, which will leave you frustrated. This frustration causes many leaders to behave in a passive-aggressive way toward people, or criticize them outright, when the reality is you set them up for failure by not making your expectations clear.

This is why the Role Description and Scorecard are so important. It is critical that as a leader you are abundantly clear about what you expect from each person you lead. If you are an employee and your leader is not providing clarity around his or her expectations of you—ask!

Nothing will create an expectations gap and all the negativity that comes with it like a lack of communication or poor communication. (Well, there is one thing—flat-out lies—but hopefully you are not in that situation.) Let's look at it from a deeply personal perspective. Do you know what your leader expects of you? Most leaders think their team members know what is expected of them, and most people think they know what their leader expects of them. Both assumptions are flawed. The result is the emergence of an expectations gap between leaders and direct reports. These can be extremely damaging to their relationship and the outcomes of their work together—but talking to each other about mutual expectations, which is real communication, leads to elevated relationships, both personally and professionally.

When you think about how important it is for each team

member to know explicitly what is expected of him or her, it is outrageous how little time and energy we spend getting this right. But here is an exercise to get you started.

Leader: Ask each direct report to take a blank sheet of paper and write down what they think you expect of them in their role.

Direct Report: Focus on the big pieces of the puzzle first. If you have room for the medium and smaller pieces, include them toward the end. When you are finished, keep a copy for yourself and give a copy to your leader.

Leader: Take a blank sheet of paper for each of your direct reports and write down what you expect of them in their role— before you look at what they wrote. Compare what you wrote with what your direct reports wrote and identify significant gaps.

Leader and Direct Report: Meet one-on-one to discuss the differences between what you each wrote.

Leader: Provide a copy of what you wrote to each direct report in these meetings.

Direct Reports: If you are also a leader, complete this exercise with your team members.

Even when very well-considered Role Descriptions and Scorecards are in place, it's amazing how gaps can develop between what you think your leader expects of you and what she actually expects of you. Every month, quarter, and year should lead to greater clarity about what is expected of every person in the organization.

Most leaders think their expectations are clear, but they aren't. If you are leading someone, it is your responsibility to ensure that that person is very clear about what you expect of him or her. You are responsible as the leader for managing and ultimately eliminating the expectations gap in this situation.

I have seen this one exercise transform teams. Knowing what your boss expects of you is so fundamental that we often overlook it. In a complex world of constant change and endless communication, it is easy to overlook the basics.

We have become hypnotized by complexity. But simplicity is the key to real innovation, success, fulfillment at work, and satisfaction with life. Even in the most complex roles and industries, simplicity is an essential component of success. Simplicity holds a power that we too often overlook or ignore.

When we act without a clear sense of mission, strategy, and culture, the chances of complicating the simple increase significantly. Make the complex simple, make the simple even simpler, and beware of people who want to complicate things.

The relationship between a leader and those he leads should be grounded in very clear expectations, with as little ambiguity and as few vagaries as possible. Clear expectations give everyone their best chance at success.

The Real Heartbreaker

The hardest expectations to meet and fulfill are the ones you don't even know about. Forget about products and customers for a minute—I have a five-year-old daughter. She has expectations of me, but many of them I would never know about if I didn't talk to her about them, asking her questions, even probing a little, because her little heart and mind may not even be able to articulate them. And even then, as hard as I try, there will still be times when she thought something was going to happen and it didn't. There is nothing quite so heart-crushing as the unmet expectation of your five-year-old little girl.

Everyone in your life has expectations of you. Boyfriend, girl-friend, husband, wife, mother, father, brothers, sisters, friends, and neighbors—everybody has expectations of you; everyone has expectations of everyone. And guess what, you have expectations of everyone in your life too. This is all natural and normal. But it is impossible to meet expectations that we don't even know exist.

And we are just talking about expectations here; we haven't even ventured into the arena of hopes and dreams. When *The Dream Manager* was first published, I was doing a workshop for a family business in California. The business had participants from three generations of the family. The grandparents had started the business, their children had carried it on, and their grandchildren were now working in it.

They were beautiful people. They were truly salt of the earth, as they say. Three generations of character on display: honest, fair, hardworking, generous, and loving—the kind of people you want to surround yourself with all the time.

During the morning session one of the exercises was to make a list of the individual dreams they had for themselves. There were about eighty family members in the room, and after they made their lists, we went around the room and I asked each person to share just one of their dreams with everyone.

As we went through the exercise, switching back and forth between generations, it became obvious they were discovering things about each other they had never known. You could tell that what different family members shared surprised the others. Finally, we made our way to the patriarch and matriarch of the family. The grandfather was a kind and gentle man, and he deferred to his wife to go first. It was clear that they had both lived rich and full lives, and I don't think anyone in the room was prepared for what was about to happen.

"When I was a little girl growing up, I never dreamed my life could have been as wonderful as it has been. We have never lived a lavish life, not because we didn't have plenty of money, but because we decided very early on in our success that simplicity was one of life's overlooked riches. So, as I sit here this morning and listen to you all speak about your hopes and dreams, I am so happy for the lives you have before you, and you know Papa and I will do anything we can to help you fulfill your dreams. For myself, my joy comes from watching you fulfill your dreams, but I do have one dream. . . ."

As she uttered these words, the room got very quiet; in fact, I am not sure I have ever seen a room get so silent so quickly. Some people leaned in and others unconsciously moved toward the edge of their seats. Then she continued, "For my whole life, I have always wanted to go to New York and see a Broadway show."

There was a collective gasp from the group. They were thinking so loudly you could hear them. How did we miss this? How is this possible? And of course, the dark realization that in all these years nobody had ever asked her what her dreams were. They looked over toward Papa, as they called him, and tears were streaming down his face. His anguished expression said, "I have failed my beloved."

One week later they had her on a plane to New York, accompanied by three of her children, five of her grandchildren, and her loving and devoted husband. She saw four Broadway shows, ate at some fabulous restaurants, and fulfilled a lifelong dream.

Here's the point. Most people have never had someone ask them what their dreams are. It is one of humanity's relationship blind spots.

Now let's turn back to the world and see how this particular aspect of the expectation and dream principles plays out at work.

Customers Have Expectations

Great teachers use a lot of questions. Great salespeople do the same.

If you are selling something, understanding the customer's expectations is essential. The problem is they are not necessarily clear about their expectations, so it is your role as the salesperson to draw them out of your customers. But depending on what you are selling, you may need to go beyond their expectations and explore their hopes and dreams for a project or product. Their dreams for a project sometimes manifest as something very specific and tangible. For example, perhaps your firm is designing and building a new office complex for a client. You may ask the CEO what her dreams are for the project, and she may say, "I want the building to have as much natural light as possible." That's a very tangible response. It is the intangible dreams that are harder to measure and therefore harder to deliver on. Take the same situation. You ask the CEO what his dreams are for the project, and he says, "My dream is for this project not to become a distraction to our business. So, I want to be involved as little as possible. Now, don't get me wrong, I am willing to be involved as much as is necessary, but if I am not adding value, I don't want to be in the meeting; I want to be focusing on moving the business forward." This is a very intangible dream, and much harder to deliver on.

Both CEOs already had these expectations and dreams for the project, but if you didn't ask you may not have known about them.

If you are selling a replacement product, there is one trap you have to be particularly careful of. I have seen this manifest in software and system upgrades almost every time an

organization undertakes such a project. The sales and project teams interview everyone, asking them what they want the new system to do that the old system doesn't do. They ask what people like and don't like about the old system or software.

The problem is people have a replacement/upgrade assumption bias. They assume that the new system or software is going to be able to do *everything* the old system did, plus new and better things. Getting beyond this assumption is essential in the project scope and design phase. In their minds, whatever you deliver is going to have their favorite features from the old system as well as everything the new system has to offer, but that is almost never true. Even if you know every single one, you still might not be able to deliver an upgraded experience in every case when it comes to all those features people loved about the old system. And if you don't know what people assume the new system will be able to do, you don't even have a chance of meeting expectations. Result: expectations gap. What fills an expectations gap? Disappointment, resentment, anger, frustration, and loss of trust.

But this is not the biggest blunder I see in the sales area when it comes to the expectations gap. Over and over throughout my career as a consultant I have seen salespeople overpromise in order to get the sale. If it is a product and the product cannot deliver on what the salesperson said it would, the reputation of the product, the trust of the customer, the character of the salesperson, and the brand of the organization are all damaged.

The Fifth Principle:
LET PEOPLE KNOW WHAT YOU EXPECT

Never lose sight of the expectations paradigm: Everybody has expectations of you, and you have expectations of everyone. This significantly impacts both our personal and professional lives. We cannot afford to be passive in this area. It is a mistake to assume that people will make their expectations clear to us. We need to be very proactive when it comes to other people's expectations, asking probing questions to get to the expectations that they may not even realize they have.

The last thing to be aware of is that not only do people have expectations of you, but you are also constantly creating expectations. As you left home this morning, perhaps your spouse asked, "What time will you be home tonight?" You said six thirty without much thought, but what have you just created? An expectation.

When there is a difference between what people expect to happen and what actually happens, an expectations gap emerges, and five things fill that gap: disappointment, resentment, anger, frustration, and loss of trust.

Do Something!

Most people are hired to do something. So do it. Get really clear about what it is and then make it happen. Become a champion of the culture, a Culture Advocate. If you have a choice between being positive and negative, choose positive. There is already enough negative in the world and in most organizations.

Everybody loves having people on their team who make things happen. Every leader loves having team members he can give work to and know he never has to think about it again, because they will get it done and done well.

How will you know if you have become a Culture Advocate? When people cannot imagine your team, department, or organization without you—then you have become a Culture Advocate.

But set that aside for now. Anything that takes us out of the present moment is fraught with danger. Culture Advocates focus on the now. Their minds are where their feet are. They ask themselves: What can I do today to make our culture more dynamic?

Think about it like this. How many people make up your organization? Twelve, two hundred, ten thousand? OK, if we multiplied your commitment to work and the culture by the number of people in your organization, what would the culture be like?

Beware of excuses. Excuses lead to inaction and mediocrity. Culture Advocates are men and women of action. They are hungry and eager to make things happen. So, do something today to improve your culture. Start with yourself: Cultivate a better attitude, do the best work you have ever done, cooperate with your colleagues, and approach your work with a sense of urgency so that if there is an unmet need you will be able to step in and make it happen. This sense of urgency will create tremendous momentum for you and your team.

Don't let what you can't do interfere with what you can do. Do something—and start today!

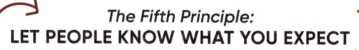

The Fifth Principle:
LET PEOPLE KNOW WHAT YOU EXPECT
(and get very clear about what is expected of you)

7

the pinnacle of culture

Listen to Your Coach, Matthew!

Most of the dominant memories of my childhood involve sports. I have seven brothers: Mark, Simon, Andrew, Brett, Nathan, Bernard, and Hamish. Growing up in Australia, all we did was play sports—any and every sport. Football, cricket, tennis, soccer, swimming, running, basketball, volleyball, golf, table tennis, biking . . . You name it, we probably gave it a try. Were we competitive? Yes, ultracompetitive. I still remember getting thrown in the pool during a cricket match in the backyard when my brothers didn't like the call. Playing sports was a way of life.

My father loved sports, and one of his favorite things to do was watch his sons play. I believe it gave him a tremendous sense of pride and filled him with great joy to watch his boys out there competing.

I began playing competitive sports when I was five years old, and my earliest memories are filled with my father's advice. Every time I went to training and every time I went to a game, my dad would say the same thing to me: "Matthew, listen to your coach!" Every time. He never forgot. If he was traveling, he would call me before a game to wish me well, and to remind me to listen to my coach.

When I was about sixteen years old, he was dropping me off for a soccer game while he went and parked the car. As I walked away from the car, he put down the window and said, "Matthew, don't forget—" I interrupted him and said, "I got it, Dad—listen to my coach, listen to my coach, listen to my coach!"

A few weeks later, Dad and I were talking and I asked him, "Dad, why do you always say, 'Listen to your coach'?"

He didn't miss a beat. He looked me straight in the eye and said, "Because nobody achieves excellence at anything without coaching."

"What do you mean?" I asked.

"You can get good at something just by working hard at it. If you've got some talent and you work hard at it, you can get really, really good at it. But excellence, peak performance, being the best you can be at something—that doesn't happen without coaching."

My father was a student of excellence. He loved excellence, wherever it could be found. He would point it out to us, in business, in sports, in the arts, in politics, spiritually and academically. He was a student of excellence, and he taught us to be students of excellence too. At the core of all excellence was his belief that coaching played an indispensable role in the life of every champion.

Coaching is the key to creating a Dynamic Culture, and the Mount Everest of leading people.

The Sixth Principle:
GROW YOUR PEOPLE BY CREATING A COACHING CULTURE

Every Leader's No. 1 Role

The role of leaders has changed radically over the past twenty years, along with almost everything else. Over and over they have been pressed with the mantra "Do more with less." Sometimes this is a good idea and can be very fruitful for a season or two, but after a decade it gets very tiresome. At that point, you simply cannot do more with less. In the same way, cost cutting is good—to a point. But I have seen too many bean counters in leadership positions who have no other tool in their belts beyond cutting costs. I have also seen them ruin great organizations and tens of thousands of people's lives. At some point the only message that gets heard is: "You people are lazy and you are wasting the organization's money." Both the "cut costs" and the "more with less" philosophy have radically altered what it means to be a leader today in practical terms.

The most important part of a team leader's role is coaching. But this aspect—the most valuable and rewarding task leaders perform—has been almost completely squeezed out of their role over the past twenty years. Some will argue that a leader's role is to decide what work needs to be done, develop systems and processes, set goals, mobilize the organization's resources to accomplish those goals, manage people to make it all happen, and measure results. I don't disagree that most of these are important aspects of a leader's role. But the best way to accomplish all of this is within the context of coaching.

A leader's No. 1 role is to coach his or her people.

The problem is that the changes within organizational life have made it so they simply don't have time for it. By constantly being asked to do more with less and cut costs, they have taken on more of the unimportant urgent things themselves, and set aside the most critical part of their role, coaching. This is one of the great tragedies in the life of modern organizations.

There was a time when we were doing more with less. Now we are doing less with less. Where are the visionary leaders who realize we can do much, much more with just a little bit more resources?

Most people need a coach much more than they need a manager. Don't get me wrong—people need to be managed. The idea of self-management is delusional and ineffective. People need help prioritizing their work in the context of the organization's overall goals, and they need to be held accountable. Without accountability, most people become the-worst-version-of-themselves. Even with a strong case for management (though as you know, I prefer to call it leadership), it remains true that the best way to manage (lead) people is to coach them.

The best leaders spend the majority of their time coaching people.

So, why don't more leaders spend more time coaching their people? Two reasons. First, they are too busy doing things that don't add value. Second, they have not been taught an effective system of coaching.

Coaching is the number one tool missing from most leaders' tool kits. I see them come to our *Don't Just Manage—Coach!* training, and within the first hour it is clear they have either never been given permission to coach or never been taught how to coach. This inevitably means their past leaders didn't coach and mentor them.

We are going to solve this problem in this chapter. You will have what you need to get started today. Will you get better over time? Absolutely. Would you benefit from our *Don't Just Manage—Coach!* training? Sure, but don't put off what you can start doing right now. Don't let what you can't do interfere with what you can do.

Some readers may be tempted to think, "Well, I'm not a manager!" or "I'm not a leader." That may be true at work. Perhaps you don't have a leadership role—yet. But we all lead people in different areas of our lives, and a coaching mentality can be a game changer. Do you lead your kids? Sure. You are constantly trying to help them realize what matters most and what matters least. Don't just tell them; coach them. Don't have kids? Fine. Do you have nieces and nephews? Do you have people come to your home to do work? When was the last time you ate in a restaurant, went out with friends, hosted a meal? We are all constantly managing people and experiences. And if you are not a leader at work, you have one. Ask your leader to coach you.

The ideas I am sharing in this chapter and throughout this book are not just for leaders. They are for every person in every organization, and they apply to both work and life.

The most important part of a leader's role is to grow people. If you want the best for your people and from your people, they need coaching. Nobody achieves excellence at anything without coaching. Without coaching, mediocrity is inevitable.

It's time to create a coaching culture in your organization, department, team, or group. *Nothing will have more impact on your culture than coaching.* It is the silver bullet of Dynamic

Cultures. Only it is not quick and easy. A culture of excellence is a coaching culture.

If you are a leader, stop thinking of yourself as a manager and start thinking of yourself as a coach. It you are bold enough, put a sign on your door that reads COACH.

Here are some quick coaching tips that you can start implementing today:

1. Make every interaction with your direct reports count. Teach them something you learned in your career, tell them a story about how you failed at something and what you learned, or show them one specific way they can become better in their role.

2. Students don't give their teachers homework to do. Don't let your people bring you half-finished work for you to complete. Coach them on what needs improving and have them try again and again, until they get it right. It is not your role to do their work.

3. Be coachable yourself. Invite your people to bring to your attention ways you can grow. If you have children, you are already well versed in how this works. They don't wait to be invited and are not suppressed by political correctness. They just tell you straight up.

4. Become a student of people. Increase your awareness of fruitful and unproductive social interactions. What is the key to becoming a great writer? People ask me this question all the time. The answer: Develop an intimate knowledge of people. What inspires and engages them? What takes the wind out of their sails and demotivates them? In art and business—and life—nothing takes the place of knowledge of the human person.

The most important piece of all this is to start to see yourself as a coach. Take coaching opportunities seriously. Never waste an opportunity, and remember coaching isn't always correction; often the most powerful words we hear from our coaches are words of encouragement. This encouragement drives engagement and enthusiasm.

Managing people isn't easy, nor is coaching. But coaching people is so much more enjoyable and rewarding than merely managing them. There is something enormously fulfilling about helping people grow. There is great satisfaction to be gained by seeing the men and women you lead accomplish things they never thought possible because you coached and encouraged them.

Coaching people means knowing them. People are different. Every one of us unique, and yet there are things we all have in common. A coach strengthens for the good of both the person and the team.

We live in a society that places an extraordinarily high value on self-expression. I am all for self-expression, but there is something more important: creating selves that are worth expressing. A great coach helps you develop the-best-version-of-yourself, the self that everyone in your life needs you to be.

As a Coaching Leader and Culture Advocate you want to understand the very core of people first, and then work toward the periphery. There are several excellent personality models that help us to accomplish this core understanding of people. The one I have been using for twenty years is the Myers-Briggs personality inventory, but there are others out there. Pick one and use it—a lot. When you are meeting with a direct report, always have a summary of their personality type before you. Make sure they have a copy too.

I encourage team members to have personality lunches. Two people, each with a summary of the other's personality type, have lunch and discuss how they see each other's personality manifesting in the workplace for better or worse. These lunches are a cultural gem.

Beyond the personality profile models, there are endless ways to learn more about people. Paradigm after paradigm, shed light on what matters to people, what moves them, what stabilizes teams and what destabilizes them.

A couple of times a year I spend an afternoon of carefree-timelessness with my good friend Mark Kaminski. *Carefree-timelessness* is a term I coined in my book *The Seven Levels of Intimacy* to describe our need for time together without an agenda in all our relationships. Mark has a great mind and loads of experience. One of the paradigms he shared with me a few years ago that I have found both powerful and practical describes four types of people in the workplace.

1. This team member shares our values and does great work.

2. This team member shares our values but doesn't do great work.

3. This team member doesn't share our values but does great work.

4. This team member doesn't share our values and doesn't do great work.

No. 1 and No. 4 are easy to deal with. You coach No. 1 to the next level and ask her to help you coach some of the younger team members. You coach No. 4 to leave because to do anything else is to jeopardize the mission, and Mission Is King.

It is No. 2 and No. 3 who present the challenges. No. 2 may just be in the wrong role, or if he's in a growth business, the role may have outgrown his talents and abilities. In this case, the difficult decision is to demote him to vice president of sales (for example) and bring in a seasoned sales president. He may thrive in the VP role. The tougher call is when you really don't see a place in the organization because he lacks the ability to deliver the world-class results you need to be successful as a team. In this scenario, you need to let him go. This is heartbreaking for most leaders because this person may be the poster child for the culture, but still we need to remember this is work, and we are responsible for a mission. Mission Is King, and keeping this person would harm the future of the organization and everybody on the team.

The stereotypical example of No. 3 is the quarterback who has endless collisions with the law and cannot get along with his teammates or management. Remember, No. 3 doesn't share our values but does great work. When teammates don't share and celebrate the organization's values, it is usually because of some element of selfishness or self-absorption. The quarterback is a champion, but he is a cancer on the culture. Unfortunately, we know all too well how this story ends. The team keeps the quarterback because he is a champion, and the culture takes a huge hit. Other talented players and coaches leave because they refuse to work with him. Maybe, just maybe, he helps the team win a Super Bowl, but usually he doesn't, and the reason is because culture is what really matters.

If you think what happens in professional sports doesn't apply to your organization, think again. Most sales teams of twenty or more have one salesperson who is toxic. A new person joining the team cannot understand why an organization with such a fabulous overall culture tolerates such a jerk. "He hits his numbers every quarter," a colleague informs the new member of the sales team.

In this scenario the problem is that nobody has looked at the whole equation. Do the math and you will realize showing that salesperson the door is not only the best thing for your culture but also the best thing for your organization. Let me explain.

If you are selling your product to a particular client, do you allow the client to pick which salesperson they want to work with? No. You assign the salesperson. So, you have assigned Mr. Toxic Jerk to a territory or group of customers. Now, if everyone inside the organization cannot stand him, how do you think your customers feel about him? But they have no choice. If they want your product, the only person they can buy it from is Mr. Toxic Jerk.

The full equation considers all the facts. In one scenario, you send a halfway decent human being who embodies your Dynamic Culture to call on the same customers, and you sell twice as much product to those customers. In another, you send Mr. Toxic Jerk, and while the customers may begrudgingly buy your product because there is demand, they might also push your competitor's product to their customers because they despise working with Mr. Toxic Jerk. In yet another scenario, your competitors come up with a product that is just as good as yours and send a delightfully charming salesperson who is eager to serve to call on the your customers. How much of your current sales might you lose?

Ultimately, you will discover that over time great salespeople begin to leave for different departments or even other organizations. Their exit interviews reveal that they simply got sick of having to work alongside this completely self-interested, self-absorbed, self-congratulatory moron.

The point is, while Mr. Toxic Jerk is hitting his numbers, it is costing you much more than it is helping you. You may not know exactly how much, but it is costing you. So dig deep, find your courage, and show Mr. Toxic Jerk the door. Will it be easy? No. The twos and threes will have you tossing and turning at night. You just have to remember, Mission Is King.

A leader's role is to grow people, and coaching is the best way to do it. Let's revisit the FLOYD philosophy for a moment: "Your organization can only become the-best-version-of-itself to the extent that the people who are driving your organization are becoming better-versions-of-themselves." Nothing will help your people become better-versions-of-themselves faster than consistent coaching.

Great leaders have great coaches, and they are great coaches. I'm not talking about good or even above-average leaders, but the truly great. Great leaders value and demand coaching.

If you are a leader and you have never had a great Coaching Leader as a boss, I highly recommend you consider entering into a coaching relationship yourself.

If you are not a leader and you don't have a great Coaching Leader or mentor in your life, you should enter into a coaching relationship too. Before I had my first executive/business/life coach, I thought coaching was a fad, all hype. But it changed my life, both personally and professionally, and it will change yours.

Most people don't have anyone in their life who they can say anything to without fear of being judged. We all need that. Most people don't have anyone in their life who can help them think systematically through their biggest challenges. We all need that. Most people don't have anyone who holds them accountable for their hopes and dreams. We all need that. Most people don't have anyone who is an expert at challenging them in ways that bring out their best. We all need that.

Coaching has made me a better person, a better leader, a better thinker, and a better writer, and it has improved my quality of life in too many ways to list. I will always have a coach, for the rest of my life.

Everybody needs a coach. Nobody goes to the Olympics without one. So, as far as I am concerned, anyone who wants to be excellent at anything should have a coach. And if nothing else, we should all want to live excellent lives filled with passion and purpose. Tell me what you want to be excellent at and I will tell you who your coach should be.

The Corporate F-Word

I've had a great life filled with incredible people and fabulous opportunities. So I don't envy many people. I do envy professional athletes. Not for any of the usual reasons, but because they *always* know how they are doing. All they need to do is look up and there it is—the scoreboard, filled with scores and stats. Once each player comes off the field, there are a dozen television shows dissecting his performance not just today, but compared with last week, last season, and his career stats. Professional athletes always know where they stand. People need that. They deserve it.

One thing that I have become absolutely convinced of: People deserve to know where they stand.

In the corporate world, we use different tools to communicate this to employees, but our main tool is the annual review. Now, let me say this clearly so that it is absolutely impossible for you not to understand what I am saying. *The annual review is a dinosaur. It's an absolute waste of time.* It's a joke. It doesn't work. Leaders are only about 60 percent honest, depending on their mood that particular day or the pressure on their schedule. Annual reviews simply *don't work* because they are too infrequent to work in any coaching capacity. *Abolish the annual review.*

How long would a football coach at your favorite college last if he reviewed player performance only once a year? Now, some will argue that a leader is constantly meeting with her or his people. True, but what do they talk about? They talk about the work.

Now, forgive me, but I am going to have to use the f-word. It is essential to the review process and critical for becoming a Coaching Leader: feedback. A coaching relationship thrives when leaders are comfortable giving feedback and team members are comfortable receiving it. Giving and receiving feedback is uncomfortable. For whatever reason, human beings don't love either of these things. At some level, we are all a little conflict averse. There is a peacemaker in all of us. Most people don't like rocking the boat.

Newsflash: You are not going to get really good at giving feedback if you do it only once a year. And guess what, the people you lead are not going to get good at receiving feedback if they get it only once a year. But the real problem is they are not going to get really good at their roles if you give them feedback only once a year.

Creating a coaching culture begins with shortening the feedback loop. Giving and receiving feedback needs to become a natural and normal part of the interaction between leaders and their team members. It should be expected and welcomed, not a surprise. We get good at giving and receiving feedback by doing these things often, just like with most other things.

Here's the good news. The review concept provides the perfect format and platform for coaching and feedback. So, we can use it—we just need to use it more than once a year.

Performance reviews are a great first step. They are an effective way to ease into a coaching relationship and let your people know that things are changing around here. The first thing you will hear is: "But our performance reviews are usually in . . ." You may even want to get ahead of that and tell your team that you have been convinced that annual reviews are a dinosaur and that from now on everyone will have a quarterly review. Let them know that this is the first step. Tell them you want to create a vibrant coaching culture and that from now on they can expect regular feedback.

This is the review process we recommend:

- A new employee has a review after thirty days.
- From then on until the end of the world an employee has a review every ninety days.
- The review consists of six questions, which are mostly used to frame a coaching conversation:
  1. During the past three months what has been working well?
  2. To be your best, what do you need to get better at?
  3. How do you feel your overall performance reflects these three qualities: committed, coachable, and aware?
  4. What are your key objectives for the next ninety days?
  5. What have you done to improve the culture in the past ninety days?
  6. Is there anything else you would like to share or discuss?

- The person being reviewed responds in writing to these five questions, and gives them to their leader one week prior to their scheduled review.
- The leader also completes the questions to note his or her observations of the employee over the past ninety days. It is preferable to do this before looking at the employee's comments.
- The Coaching Leader and employee meet for no more than one hour to have a very open and honest conversation about what is working and what is not.
- Each person then signs the review notes. Each person receives a copy, and a copy is placed in the employee's file.

One of the primary purposes of the review process is to let people know clearly where they stand. People deserve that. Don't avoid the tough conversations. People deserve to know the ways they are succeeding, and where they are falling short or even outright failing. Not to tell them is at the very least unfair, but more than that, it is cowardly. If you don't tell them, you are essentially inviting them to play a game in which you decide who wins or loses while refusing to tell them the rules. The problem is, the game is their career—so it is no game at all. This is serious stuff, because behind that word *career* are real people and real things such as feeding and educating children, paying the mortgage, the family's annual vacation, and saving for retirement.

Just before you end each review, pause for a moment and ask yourself: What have I not said because I am too much of a coward? Make it part of your process. You can say to your direct report, "While we are here, let's just take a moment quietly to ourselves to think about if there is anything that we have left unsaid that needs to be said." They are most likely not saying something that they should be sharing with you also.

As you become a Coaching Leader, the employee quarterly performance review will be the central formal coaching experience. But by having these review sessions, you also change the nature of every informal conversation you have each day with your people. The formal review sessions and the informal conversations create an environment of continuous coaching. Any truly professional environment is one of continuous learning and continuous coaching. The best of the best always have coaches, and champions love coaching.

Coaching leads to excellence. If we want our people to be excellent, coaching is a natural next step. We cannot reasonably expect our people to grow if we do not coach them.

This review process actually becomes a delightfully simple and effective built-in coaching system. So, for anyone who wants to become a Coaching Leader, it is a great starting point. This one change to the way you run your team or organization would be an enormous first step toward creating a coaching culture.

It is also worth noting one more time that for the best leaders, the coaching aspect of their role is the most rewarding part of their work. As a result, as we have squeezed coaching out of the role of most managers (leaders), not only have we have robbed them of the very natural fulfillment that comes from helping people grow, but we have also attracted the wrong people to leadership as a result—people who have no interest in helping others grow. In many cases they don't even enjoy people. How can you be a great leader if you don't like people?

At the core of every authentic leader is a desire to help each person become the-best-version-of-themselves, so that the organization can become the-best-version-of-itself. You have to care about the people and the organization to accomplish the mission.

Coaching is the future of leading people. It is the most effective way to achieve all our business goals. Here are ten coaching tips to keep in mind as you embark on this incredibly rewarding journey:

1. **BE HONEST.** Don't hold back. Be honest with people. Tell them the good, the bad, and the ugly—then remind them of the good again. People need and deserve to know exactly where they stand. Honesty is the most admired quality in a leader. Be candid and kind, be direct, and stick to the facts.

2. **PRIORITIZE COACHING.** Make your coaching sessions a priority. Don't blow them off, and don't let the participant blow them off. Coaching is your number one priority as a leader.

3. **CONNECT.** Begin by establishing a connection. Allow them to know who you really are as a person. Share what's important to you. Not all at once, but little by little over time. And above all communicate that you have the person's best interest at heart—that you want to help them grow and succeed. Do it naturally. Talk about what you did or are going to do on the weekend, favorite foods, teams you follow, what you are reading.

4. **PREPARE.** Make sure you know before the meeting exactly what you want them to work on, or how you want them to grow and improve. This matters regardless of the length of the meeting; it could be five minutes or an hour.

If you don't give them something to work on, you are telling them that you are 100 percent satisfied with everything they do and there is no way for them to improve.

5. **EXPLAIN WHAT AND WHY.** Coaching allows you to teach the why, not just the what. Leaders often have to ask people to do things, but they don't have the time to explain why that task or project matters. Coaching allows you to explain the why. This helps raise up future strategic leaders, because the strategy is usually locked up in the why. It also passes on valuable institutional knowledge. Get beyond tasks and instructions, and really help people understand why we do things, and why we do them a certain way. Understanding the why allows people to make mission king more than ever before, and inspires them to commit to that mission more than ever before.

6. **ASK.** The very best coaches use questions to teach powerfully. Get really good at asking questions. Don't tell them everything. Allow them to propose and initiate the solution. Ask questions that lead them to where they need to go, and then allow them to figure it out for themselves. A great question to start each session with is: What are you hoping to get out of this session today? or, What would be most helpful for us to work on today?

7. **LISTEN.** Don't do all the talking. Great coaches are really good listeners.

8. **INVITE FEEDBACK.** Invite your participant to give you feedback. Don't take it personally. Ego is the enemy of coachability. If it is good feedback, live it. Thank them for the feedback, more than once. It is extremely uncomfortable for people to give their boss feedback.

9. **ENCOURAGE.** I'm good at what I do. My books have

sold more than thirty-five million copies, but there are still days when I am filled with self-doubt when I sit down to write. We never outgrow the need to be encouraged. So be sure to take every chance you get to encourage your team members.

10. THIS IS A GIFT. Coaching is an incredible gift. Let those you coach know that this will serve them well not just at work, but in every area of their lives—and not just now, at this organization, but for the rest of their lives wherever they go. Don't be embarrassed to say that you are intentionally investing in them with the hope that they will invest in others to help them grow.

Dynamic Cultures are coaching cultures, and coaching cultures have epic levels of engagement. Nothing will more radically increase employee engagement than coaching. What is a coaching culture? It's a culture in which coaching is a natural and normal part of every day. It is an organization where coaching is encouraged, desired, contagious, and celebrated. A culture of coaching is a culture of excellence.

When you are actively coaching your people, mediocrity has nowhere to hide. When you stop relying on hearsay to lead your team, a disengaged employee cannot hide behind the rest of the team's work. Coaching makes you aware of things you would never be aware of otherwise. There is simply no better way to really understand your people and what they are capable of contributing.

Coaching is also the only truly effective way to offer career development and career pathing. The coaching relationship allows both coach and employee to explore strengths and weaknesses, and to evaluate any skills gap that would prevent someone from achieving their career goals. Coaching is the ultimate career development.

The quarterly review alone is a game changer when it comes to professional development. But by raising Coaching Leaders, you take professional development into the stratosphere.

Grow your people by leading them well and coaching them. Coaching demonstrates that you are interested in employees not only as employees but also as human beings—living, breathing people, who have lives and families beyond the confines of the corporate offices. Coaching is an honest investment in your people, and it will bear astounding fruits in every area from engagement to innovation.

What does your organization's professional development system look like? Not what the brochure or employee manual says, but in reality. Notice I didn't say professional development *program*. You don't need a program; you need a system.

FLOYD has been helping organizations of all sizes develop Professional Development Systems (PDS) for longer than I can remember. There are a handful of key components to a PDS, but nothing is more important than coaching. Raise up Coaching Leaders or hire external coaches for your people— or do both. Nothing is more powerful than coaching when it comes to developing your people.

The most common excuse for not investing in people is also the worst excuse. Time and again I hear business leaders and business owners saying, "Well, 40 percent of them won't stay, so what's the point investing in them in such powerful ways?"

This is insanity. Whether they stay or leave is irrelevant, primarily because developing people is one way a business contributes to society. Developing people in these ways raises up better parents and lovers; coaches for our children's soccer teams; better board members and volunteers for local charities; and the list goes on. The positive repercussions of coaching your people are endless.

This perception that many of your employees will leave is also lunacy purely from a business point of view. First, coaching alone will reduce the number of really talented people who leave your organization and increase the number of mediocre people who leave. Mediocrity hates accountability. Second, coaching drives individual and team engagement through the roof. Third, even if someone great does leave to pursue his dream career somewhere else, he will be a fabulous ambassador for your organization forever. This is beneficial for your brand in every way, and it will attract other great talent to your door. And finally, the work product they create while they are with you will be vastly superior than if you didn't invest in them.

If you really want to contribute to society as an organization, stop making those charitable contributions to causes you are probably not even passionate about and that you feel obliged to make for your corporate image—and instead invest in your people. Take 1 to 3 percent of payroll and commit it to developing your people as a line item in the budget.

Invest in your people. Grow your people. Nothing is better for business and society than developing people, and the best way to develop them is with coaching. Every coaching participant becomes a coach for others in his or her life. And everybody needs a coach.

Create a coaching culture. There is nothing you can do that will have more impact on your organization.

A coaching culture has a fast feedback loop. This will benefit an organization as it strives to bring out the best in its people, but it also overflows into a dozen different areas. A faster feedback loop in the arena of product development can be priceless. In a culture where people get comfortable giving and receiving feedback, a lot of inefficiency and waste are eliminated.

One other thing: If you decide to build the committed, coachable, and aware framework into your team or organization, bring everything back to these qualities. Praise participants when they display these behaviors, and challenge them when they fall short. Integrate the three qualities into formal and informal conversations every day, so that the language permeates the culture.

You can start creating a coaching culture today. You don't need to get permission. Who can argue with you investing in your people? Give it a try. Go rogue. See what happens. Everybody has a dozen opportunities, personally and professionally, to coach other people. Start boldly embracing those opportunities.

It doesn't matter where people are in their careers or lives. It matters where you take them, and it is your role to take them there. It is your responsibility to grow your people.

You're ready. Start coaching your people. It will be one of the most rewarding experiences of your life.

The Currency of Great Leaders

You will learn so much about your people by coaching them. You will gain a completely new appreciation of their strengths and weaknesses, which will allow you to deploy them with ever-increasing effectiveness. But that is just the tip of the iceberg.

The first thing you will discover is just how coachable your people are. This one data point tells you a tremendous amount about a person. People who are coachable tend to be hungry for best practices and committed to continuous learning. These types of people are always going to run circles around their competition. Champions love coaching. Never forget this. People who resist coaching are unlikely to become champions. The best want to get better. They crave coaching.

Coaching will also make you phenomenal at hiring new team members. It is a horrible thing to have to let someone go. It hurts the employee and his family, it impacts team morale, and it keeps you awake at night. We should do everything we can to avoid ever making a hiring mistake. By coaching your people and learning about how they learn, grow, give and receive feedback, and so many other things, you will constantly be refining what makes a great member of your team.

Over time you will discover that people really do fall into the four categories we discussed earlier. Two of these groups are very easy to deal with, while the other two can cause considerable challenges to an organization and its leadership. Remember, they are categorized according to values and work.

- **Category 1:** This team member shares our values and does great work. EASY. Action: Encourage and empower her.

- **Category 2:** This team member shares our values but is not doing good work. CHALLENGING. Action: Take an honest, objective look at the role this person is doing and ask yourself if he is in the right role for his strengths and talents. If you determine that he is not in the right role and another role that appears to be a better fit is available, consider moving him to that role. At every step the employee deserves to know exactly where he stands. If another role is not available or he is given a chance in another role and fails, invite him to leave.

- **Category 3**: This team member doesn't share our values, but is performing his or her work at an extraordinary level. VERY DIFFICULT. What to do? You know what to do, but you will struggle with it every single time.
- **Category 4**: This team member doesn't share our values and doesn't contribute good work. EASY. Action: Invite him or her to leave.

Consider the case of the salesperson we discussed, Mr. Toxic Jerk. Most organizations look at the numbers and conclude they have to keep him because they can't afford to lose the sales revenue. This is horrible logic. So they tolerate this cancer in their culture, and the more they tolerate it, the worse it becomes.

The problem is they based their whole action plan on a false assumption. They assumed they were going to lose the sales. But even if they replaced that salesperson with someone really average, the new salesperson would at least get some sales. Let's assume Mr. Toxic Jerk had a remarkable gift, but you find someone with both solid experience and a good track record. This new salesperson retains 80 percent of Mr. Toxic Jerk's accounts and market share. What would you do now? Is it worth 20 percent to restore health to the organization's culture?

But we still have not considered all the factors. We still don't have the full picture. We have not done the math that really counts.

As we discussed, most organizations do not send salespeople to audition for a client and then let the client choose which salesperson they wish to work with. Organizations dictate to clients what salesperson they *must* order from in most cases. In the case of Mr. Toxic Jerk, considering nobody internally can stand to even be in the same room with him, how do you think your clients feel about him? Most organizations don't know. The client doesn't have a choice, so they keep buying from the toxic jerk because your product is good until something and someone better comes along.

Now suppose your competitor sends a reasonably talented salesperson who is also a halfway decent human being to call on the same customers. How much business will you lose? And next, let's suppose that the same organization comes up with a halfway decent product, as competitors have the nasty little habit of doing. And suppose they now send that half-decent product with that half-decent salesperson to call on the customers the toxic jerk is servicing. How much business will you lose then?

Did I just tell the same story in different ways two chapters in a row? *Yes!* Am I losing my mind? *No!* This is that important. It never pays to allow cancer in your culture.

Have you ever wondered how cancer starts? I'm probably more interested than most because I was diagnosed with three different types of cancer before I was forty years old. Let me tell you something—that will get your attention. Anyway, your body has one hundred million cells (macro). Cancer begins by inducing change in one cell (micro). This single cell grows too fast, multiplies, and now you have a small group of cancerous cells. Still a micro problem, especially if it's discovered early enough.

Cancer kills people and it kills cultures. We've all seen it kill people, and if we reflect, we have probably all seen it kill team cultures and the cultures of whole organizations. Cancer is not a joke. If your doctor told you tomorrow that you had cancer and explained the different types of treatment available, you wouldn't casually say, "Thanks, doc. Let me think about that, and we will deal with it when things slow down a bit at work." There is only one way to deal with cancer: aggressively. You have to locate it, determine how much it has spread, and cut it out. Culture cancer needs to be dealt with in exactly the same way.

If that cancer were in your body, you would attack it with vigor. You would cut it out, banish it. You would have no tolerance for it. You wouldn't think about how long you could live with it before getting rid of it. You would act swiftly and decisively. We should act in exactly the same way when it comes to culture cancer. Culture cancer is always life-threatening to your organization.

There are times when you need to let people go. Once you realize that, act upon it. It doesn't serve anyone to drag it out. Don't deceive yourself—you usually know quickly. Don't pretend. And remember, every firing decision is a hiring decision: If you were hiring this person today rather than firing him, knowing everything you know today, would you hire him? Or if a team member came to your office tomorrow morning and told you that she had been offered a role with another organization and she had decided to take it, how would you feel? Would you feel relieved? Or would you feel panicked, knowing you absolutely could not afford to lose that person because she is indispensable to the success of your team and organization?

Success favors the bold. Once you have the information you need to make a decision, act decisively.

If an organization is weak in dealing with cancer in the culture or people who are a bad fit for the team, it is a sign that something is wrong. The number one leadership quality missing in the corporate world today is *managerial courage*. It has become disturbingly rare among leaders.

Managerial courage is a three-step process of accountability that Coaching Leaders use to achieve extraordinary results. Here are the steps:

Step 1: Expect

A leader should expect good things from his people, but it is unreasonable to expect things from your people if you have not made your expectations clear. As we discussed briefly in relation to the expectations gap, most people have no idea what their leader expects of them. The first step in the process is to make your expectations of a person, team, or project abundantly clear.

Step 2: Inspect

A leader should regularly inspect her people and projects. Inevitably when she does so, she will discover some things that need improvement or are just plain wrong. Whenever possible, these inspections should be regular and scheduled, rather than a surprise, which tends to make people anxious and paranoid.

Step 3: Coach

Having made his expectations clear, performed a regular inspection, and discovered some opportunities for improvement, a leader now coaches the person or team to close that gap between what he expects and what he discovered during the latest inspection.

Why don't most leaders practice managerial courage? The truth is, it takes a lot of time, effort, and energy to get very clear about what we expect. Whether those expectations are for a particular team member or an entire project, it is real work to get clear about what we expect. This is why, astoundingly, many leaders cannot get together a Role Description that even vaguely reflects the role. Leaders are busy doing all the wrong things. They are exhausted because the soulful part of their role has been exiled in favor of work that drains their energy.

This is the same reason leaders tend not to have regularly scheduled inspections. Sure, they have the occasional accidental inspection, but this manifests in them hearing something from someone that is completely out of context and losing their head over it, or stumbling over some work product on the way out of the office one night that he or she is dissatisfied with. It takes effort, intentionality, discipline, and energy to regularly inspect your people and projects. The ninety-day review process will satisfy the people piece, and perhaps you need something similar for big projects—a ninety- or even a thirty-day project review.

And finally, if you are not in the habit, it takes a lot of energy to coach your team and close the gap between where they are and where you expect them to be. But find a Team Leader who gets energy and joy from coaching his people and you will have found the leader of the future.

Step one is addressed with a Role Description and Scorecard that are practical and real, which evolve through the ninety-day review process. Steps two and three are dealt with formally via the quarterly review process, and informally through daily organic conversations between a Coaching Leader and her team members.

Managerial courage is essential to a coaching culture, and coaching is essential to a Dynamic Culture. It all ties together and is essential to long-term success.

The secret to establishing this kind of culture and developing managerial courage is something that I have hinted at a few times throughout the book. It is one of the most important lessons I have learned in my career. I was familiar with the idea, but it had never really clicked with me. It was an HR leader who finally got it through my very thick skull.

I was in the boardroom with the leadership team of a very successful nonprofit that was experiencing massive growth, and a difficult decision needed to be made. There was George Josten, a twenty-nine-year-old HR professional. I don't use that word, *professional*, lightly. He is a consummate professional. George was there to answer any HR-related questions the leadership team might have as they worked their way through the problem at hand.

The conversation rambled around the room, moving from salient points that needed to be considered to a clear discomfort with the decision that everyone knew needed to be made and acted upon expediently.

I turned to George, who is always the quiet observer, taking in all the data and other people's perspectives before offering his thoughts, and asked, "What are your thoughts?"

"It seems that some of you are trying to get comfortable with this. The thing I would say is that you are probably never going to get comfortable with it, but don't forget, he has put you in this situation. You hired him to do something very specific, which he said he could do, and he has failed to do it. Now you need to let him go, and you are trying to get comfortable with that. You are not supposed to be comfortable with some of this stuff. Your discomfort points to an emotional intelligence that probably makes you very, very good at serving this organization. The goal here is to make the right decision. The goal is not to get comfortable. You are a relatively new leadership team and these things are going to come up from time to time. They do even in the best organizations. You have to get comfortable being uncomfortable."

Wow. I just sat there. Twenty-nine years old. "You have to get comfortable being uncomfortable." Brilliant. Powerful and practical. At once he told them it's OK to be uncomfortable and you should be. But at the same time, you have to be OK with being uncomfortable and do what needs to be done.

It was one of the best moments on a team ever. I talk about it all the time. If you want to be a good leader, coach, parent, spouse, friend, and so on, the faster you get comfortable being uncomfortable, the better.

Managerial courage just might be the art of getting comfortable being uncomfortable. What I am certain of is this: If we want to build a Dynamic Culture, we all need to get comfortable being uncomfortable. A Culture Advocate celebrates mission as king even when it is uncomfortable.

But to accomplish all this, you need plenty of the currency of great leaders. Again, it doesn't matter if you are a leader or a team member in your organization. Everybody needs this currency.

Let me set this up by sharing a little something about myself. I am a massive introvert, so a crowd of people in a social setting is a form of torture for me. Small talk is another form of torture. So I have developed a number of questions for situations like these to make them more enjoyable and to avoid appearing completely awkward.

One of my favorite questions is: What are you reading at the moment? There are so many books I'd like to read, and it gets harder and harder to know which books to invest my time in. So I love it when people share with me what they are reading and the most salient points. A five-minute conversation might save me five hours of reading. I love books, but there are just too many to read in one lifetime, so hearing about what other people are reading is very helpful. I used to like asking people what their favorite book was, but with success that became embarrassing because some people thought I wanted them to say one of my books, and others' favorite book actually was one of mine. So, sadly, I have had to retire that question.

Another one of my favorite questions to ask people, both socially and when I am interviewing them for a role in one of my organizations, is: Who is the best boss you've ever had? Get people talking about the best boss, leader, coach, or teacher they ever had and you are always inspired. The incredible gratitude that people have for these men and women who have touched their lives so deeply always impacts me.

There is something else I have noticed. There seem to be two universal themes that flow through these stories when people talk about the most influential teacher, coach, leader, or boss in their lives.

The first is "tough but fair." The great influencers of our lives tend to be tough but fair. They push us. They encourage and empower us to explore parts of ourselves we didn't even know existed. They stretch us—so much so, there may be times when we are not sure if they love us or hate us. But it is the fairness that makes the toughness work: "I always knew my boss had my best interest at heart." This is what allows them to push us so hard. We know they only want us to become the-very-best-version-of-ourselves.

The alchemy of mentoring combines these two qualities to create the essential quality of great leaders: respect. Respect is the currency that great leaders trade in, and it is beyond trust.

Trust is just permission to play. You cannot lead without trust. You can't even have functioning relationships without it. But respect takes your leadership to a whole new level, as well as your relationships, both personal and professional.

If people respect you, they will push themselves harder and faster when you need them to. Without respect, it is impossible to create and lead a dynamic team.

This is why it doesn't matter if you are a leader or a team member when it comes to so much of what we are discussing here. Take respect as a specific example. First, it is not something you can start developing when you become a leader. You have to develop it long before you become a leader. Second, respect is an essential element in all dynamic relationships. What happens when lovers lose respect for each other? At the core of great marriages is mutual respect. It's difficult enough to parent children, but imagine trying to parent if you have done something offensive enough to lose your child's respect. Respect is at the center of all great relationships. Have you ever had to work for a boss you don't respect? That is torture.

The thing about respect is that by the time you need it, it's too late to start developing it. The seed needs to be planted long before. A tree with strong roots can weather any storm, but when the storm arrives, it's too late to sink the roots. When the storm blows through, you either have the roots or you don't.

Respect is one of the strong roots of leadership, and one of the strong roots of every great Coaching Leader. Without it people will not follow you, and they will not sweat for you, never mind bleed for you. Nothing will help you build respect like the regular and respectful practice of managerial courage as a powerful coaching tool.

Great cultures are built on respect too. The collective respect for leaders, customers, clients, teams, and the work itself all come together to form a culture worthy of respect, or not. Is your culture worthy of respect? If you don't like the answer to that question, be a Culture Advocate and do something about it. Start today.

Ignatius of Loyola said, "Pray as if everything depends on God, but work as if everything depends on you." Culture Advocates who are not leaders hope that their leaders will become Culture Advocates, but they are not waiting for them to come around to that. Culture Advocates set out to create a Dynamic Culture with the determination of someone who believes it depends entirely on them.

Everything is a function of both formal and informal leadership. Organizations that commit to raising up Coaching Leaders who are comfortable being uncomfortable, committed to helping their people become the-best-version-of-themselves by exercising managerial courage, and broadly respected will always develop Dynamic Cultures.

The Coaching Trap

The great temptation when it comes to coaching is to cross a line that once crossed is very difficult to reestablish. This line exists between empowerment and entitlement. The role of a coach is to encourage and empower those he or she is coaching.

At FLOYD we have Executive Coaches, Business Coaches, Sales Coaches, Life Coaches, and of course we have plenty of Dream Managers. There is one thing I say to them all over and over again: "Avoid the trap." Sometimes I have to say to one of them, "You fell into the trap, didn't you?" They know it and I know it when it happens. And that coach will sheepishly reply, "Yep!"

It can happen so easily. You are the Coaching Leader of a reasonably talented team member, and he takes advantage of the coaching part of your relationship to ask for a favor that he otherwise would not have been able to request. It could be something as simple as asking for extra time off, or information about an important announcement in advance. It usually starts with something small; if the request were too large, you would turn it down immediately. The problem is that the small request starts you down a very slippery slope that sooner or later will have you crossing that line—and right on the other side of that line is the trap.

The thing you have to keep in mind is that very rarely do coaches actually create an attitude of entitlement in someone they are coaching. The entitlement is usually already there; the coach simply allows it to come to life in the coach-participant relationship. So one of the best ways to avoid the trap is to be aware of signs of entitlement in order to spot them early.

The definition of *entitlement* in this context is "the belief that one inherently deserves special treatment or privileges." We all have traces of this quality, and we have all seen it in its ugliest extremes, either in real life or on television. Like any vice, it starts small and grows, but here are some signs that you may have someone particularly entitled on your team.

1. Entitled people play by their own set of rules. They are comfortable with double standards and don't expect the rules that apply to everyone else (for example, showing up for work on time or working one's way up from the bottom) to apply to them.

2. Entitled people disrespect the common good. For instance, they carelessly throw trash on the floor or put their feet and dirty shoes up on a chair that someone is obviously going to sit on before too long.

3. Entitled people often see teammates as competitors in an unhealthy, binary, zero-sum way.

4. Entitled people are takers. The world is full of givers and takers, and takers find it very hard to give. For example, different team members volunteer each week to bring in cookies or doughnuts each Friday, but the entitled person never volunteers. They are freeloaders.

5. Entitled people feel massively put upon when you ask even the smallest favor of them, but they expect you to make any favor they might request a priority and consider it only a small request.

6. Entitled people are unaware. They are oblivious to how their behavior impacts others. For example, they repeatedly cancel appointments or make plans with friends and then cancel at the last moment. It never occurs to them that their friends might have changed their own plans to accommodate them to begin with. The simple truth is they don't care.

7. Entitled people are manipulative. They will do almost anything to get what they want. (Beyond the entitled there is another category of people called narcissists, who will in fact do *anything* to get what they want, but the narcissist has a handful of antisocial and self-destructive qualities beyond entitlement). But the entitled person will lie in a way that disparages a colleague to get ahead.

8. Entitled people think they are better or more important than other people. This may have been spawned by a

parent or grandparent who constantly told them they were special or simply by attending an elite school.

9. Entitled people look out only for themselves. They expect their needs—and often their wants—to be given priority over the needs of others. And they will often go to great lengths to ensure that they are.

10. Entitled people find it very difficult to compromise. For example, they feel like Italian food, but everyone else wants to go for Chinese food, and yet they insist on going for Italian food. Similarly, they are horrible to negotiate with because they simply believe that everyone should give them what they want.

11. Entitled people will punish you when you don't give them what they want. The punishment can take many forms: verbal abuse, ignoring you or giving you the silent treatment, gossiping about you, sabotaging a project you are working on, or blocking an initiative you favor. Entitled people never run out of ways to punish you if you don't do what they want or give them what they want.

12. Entitled people take credit for other people's work. For example, when they work on a team they often automatically consider themselves to be the leader, regardless of whether that is based in any notion of reality. And when the team's project is finished, they will take a disproportionate amount of the credit. (There is that word again: *take*.) They also blame the rest of the team, refusing to take responsibility personally when a project goes wrong.

13. Entitled people expect everyone else to be more interested in what's important to them than they are ever interested in what matters to someone else. As a result, they make for very difficult friends, lovers, parents, and colleagues.

Are there more entitled people in the workforce today than there were twenty, fifty, a hundred years ago? Yes, yes, and yes. People expect more from work today than ever before. More than a paycheck and benefits, younger generations want their work to be fun or meaningful or self-aggrandizing. They are also impatient—the natural result of growing up in a culture in which instant gratification isn't fast enough—and so we should not be surprised to discover that they want things now and are often unwilling to pay their dues. Some of their expectations may be reasonable, and others may be unreasonable. How do we know which are which? Mission Is King—those expectations that help you fulfill your mission more effectively are the ones to focus on.

Managing the entitled will be a subject unto itself over the next twenty years.

We should always be on the lookout for entitlement in ourselves, and we should continually beware of entitlement in other people, because letting people like that too close to us is dangerous. As a Coaching Leader you also need to keep an eye out for the entitled direct report. It is something to be mindful of in the interview process as well. Is it difficult to schedule time with a candidate? Does a potential candidate seem more interested in what's in it for him than how he can add value to your team? Do you see any signs of elitism, superiority, or selfishness? Does the candidate make unusual requests or demands? Entitlement is a finely honed form of selfishness, but it is very difficult to hide from the trained eye.

What do you do if you have an entitled member on your team? I'll tell you what I've been telling you all along: Grow your people. Every person you coach, every person you lead has a unique area in which they need to grow right now. They may need to grow in many areas, but this is the area you both need to focus on right now. The Coaching Leader is able to identify and isolate that need. This doesn't mean you ignore every aspect of the person's life and career, but by helping them move forward in that one area you will ensure that they will make all sorts of progress in every area of their lives.

In the case of the entitled person, I will warn you from the start that they are almost incurable. I say "almost" because I hope they can change, but I have never seen it happen. What I know for sure is that entitlement is a very dangerous form of culture cancer. The behavior of any team member infected with the cancer of entitlement needs to be courageously addressed. Give them a chance to change, but if they don't, invite them to leave. Protect your king by protecting your culture.

As a Coaching Leader, if you end up face-to-face with an entitled direct report, this essential teaching about mission is at the heart of emotional intelligence. The entitled person has both very high and very low EQ. Their high EQ is on display in their ability to manipulate people and situations. This is the dark side of the gift. They have low EQ in that they lack awareness, which manifests particularly in their inability to see things from another person's perspective. But more important and most specifically, the entitled person lacks the ability to see things from another person's perspective. They either cannot or will not imagine what it feels like to be on the other side of their behavior. Simply put, they lack empathy. As a Coaching Leader you should constantly be trying to get the entitled team member to put himself or herself in other people's shoes.

Any coach who encounters the entitled person should focus on helping him or her to develop the positive side of EQ—that is, the emotional intelligence that makes us aware of how the things we do and say affect other people, and allows us to alter our behavior to create healthier relationships.

This awareness is best awakened with questions. Direct comments will only awaken long-established defense mechanisms in the entitled that prevent them from hearing anything you say. Any one of the preceding thirteen points gives birth to a dozen such questions. For example, in relation to number four, you might ask: Who are three people who are more generous than you? Why do you think they are more generous? Is becoming more generous important to you? Why? Why not? Do you think other people are generally more generous than you?

With each question, pose it and then wait. Let them think and respond. If they respond too quickly, they are probably reacting rather than responding. In this situation, you may want to ask for some evidence by asking something like: What makes you feel that way? Just as in the interview process, resist the temptation to end the silence by saying something. Just let the question hang there in the air to be considered. Needless to say, something like this can only be addressed after a considerable rapport has been established with trust and respect.

These things we are speaking of may seem far from the realities of personal and professional life, but that is not so. If you take the heart and soul out of the body, it will die, and the same is true for an organization. An organization can live longer without its heart and soul than a person, but the stench of impending death is noticeable to everyone who encounters the culture of that organization.

Life is messy. People are messy. Business is messy. Organizations of all types, large and small, are messy. But somehow out of all the mess we are able to make something beautiful. It is then that we realize that life is beautiful, people are beautiful, and business can and should be beautiful. And there are few things more beautiful than helping people become the-best-version-of-themselves.

So, avoid the coaching trap. Focus on empowering your people, and stay clear of the line that crosses over to the land of entitlement. It is a dysfunctional land of death and destruction.

I must say the main reason coaches cross that line is because they want good things for the person they are coaching more than that person wants it for him- or herself. "I'll just help him along a little," they say to themselves, but before they know it, they are stuck in the coaching trap of entitlement.

Like any coach, the Coaching Leader will encounter people who say they really, really want something, but their actions boldly announce the exact opposite. Trust their actions. People who are unwilling to work for the things they say are really important to them can be dangerous on a team. It's your role to coach them to align their actions with their desire for success.

The number one responsibility of any coach is to hold the participant accountable. Our society is allergic to accountability. We have all perhaps become a little entitled and little addicted to instant gratification. Our natural reaction is to shirk accountability, but we need it. We need to be held accountable. If you are a leader, your people need to be held accountable. It brings out the best in them. Can you think of any situation in which somebody was accountable to nobody and it ended well? No, nor can I. For thousands of years, wisdom writers from all traditions have been observing: *Absolutum dominium corrumpit absolute.* Absolute power corrupts absolutely. What is absolute power? Many things, I suppose, but among them it is the absence of accountability.

People need to be accountable, both personally and professionally. Will they resist it? Yes. Do we all have a little resistance to the things we know are best for us? Indeed. Do we love the people who encourage us, or inspire us, or drag us through that invisible wall of resistance? Absolutely.

This is why accountability is an essential component of leading, managing, and coaching people, and therefore at the center of what a Coaching Leader does. By holding people accountable you are helping them to build a bigger and better future, personally and professionally. You are doing them a favor, developing in them a life skill that transfers to every aspect of their life. They will thank you for it one day.

The worst coaches are those who are too nice. Nice is dangerous. Too nice is diabolical in a situation like this. It's not your role to be their friend. People don't need another friend, buddy, mate—they have friends, they have buddies, they have mates—they need a coach. Everybody does.

It takes great courage to boldly hold people accountable. It takes courage to coach, because it involves holding people accountable to what they agreed they would do. But doesn't everything worth doing? Everything in life requires courage, whether it is playing football or coaching football, crossing the room to ask a woman on a date, breaking up with someone you know is not for you, or rekindling a love that has grown cold. Whether it's your first day at college or your first day back at college after twenty years, starting a new business, battling a potentially fatal disease, getting married, struggling to overcome an addiction, or coming humbly before someone you have hurt and asking for forgiveness, life requires courage.

But so many people are entrapped by fear. Fear paralyzes the human spirit. Courage is not the absence of fear, but the acquired ability to move beyond fear. Each day we must each make our way through the jungles of self-doubt, cross the valley of fear, and climb the mountain of self-imposed limitations. Only then can we live in the high places.

Courage is essential to the human experience. It is the price life charges for success. Courage is the mother and father of every great moment and movement in history. It animates us, brings us to life, and makes possible what has always seemed impossible.

The Pinnacle of Culture

Everybody wants to work for an organization that has a great culture. If somebody doesn't want that, you don't want that person working for you. So, culture matters! How much? Only you can decide now. I have made the best case I can for making culture a top priority in your organization. Now it is up to you. How seriously are you going to take culture in the next twelve months, three years, ten years?

Throughout our time together we have covered many concepts. It is my hope that these concepts will become touchstones for you as you set out to transform your culture, and that in spending your money on this book—and more important, investing your time to read it—you have experienced indisputable value.

There are many things you can do to improve your culture, regardless of your role, and you should do these things. But each of them should take you one step closer to creating a coaching culture.

The Sixth Principle:
GROW YOUR PEOPLE BY CREATING A COACHING CULTURE

A coaching culture has both formal and informal aspects. Teaching your managers (leaders) to become Coaching Leaders is a formal aspect. The quarterly review process is also a formal aspect that will be a huge leap forward in creating a coaching culture. But there are daily informal opportunities to be a Coaching Leader.

The beautiful thing about establishing a culture of coaching is that you are unleashing the incredible power of the human spirit in unimaginable ways. The people you coach will become coaches to other people inside and outside the organization, and over time you will build a coaching culture. Furthermore, as promised, these principles apply to our personal and professional lives. For example, someone who has been coached well will use those same coaching skills as a parent and in a dozen ways we will never know about. Even in an age of advanced technology, the present and the future still belong to human potential.

An administrative assistant will bring the coaching concept to the soccer club she helps run. A business manager or CFO will bring the coaching concept to the nonprofit organization where he sits on the board. A salesperson will bring the coaching concept to the various ministry leaders at her church. A maintenance team member will bring the coaching concept to the charity he volunteers with.

The power of these concepts is that once you share them with people, you empower those same people to take them and share them with everyone who crosses their path. When we feel loved and cared for rather than threatened, our natural response as human beings is generosity. When people generously teach us life-changing ideas, our natural response is to go out and teach those same concepts to everyone in our circle of influence.

There are so many things that touch me deeply as an author. The first is when someone asks me to sign their book and they hand me this heap of worn pages that have been read so often, with notes in the margins and ideas underlined or highlighted. That's a humbling experience. Then there is the leader or business owner who tells me she bought a copy for everyone on her team. Or I visit an organization and see the ideas have been taken off the pages of my book and put into practice. These experiences send a chill through my bones as an author and remind me of the mind-blowing responsibility I have to carefully craft the words and ideas I put on these pages.

I hope I have given you another book worthy of these things.

Whether you are the CEO of a Fortune 500 company, a small-business owner, the pastor of a church, leader of a nonprofit, a professional football coach, or just working on the front lines of a business or organization, do something today to put one idea from this book into action in your life and at your organization.

Don't fall into the trap of thinking you need some elaborate plan before you can start. You don't. That is a delay tactic. Begin today.

Over time it would be great to develop a culture plan. We at FLOYD would love to help you do that. But before you do, put all your managers (leaders) through the *Don't Just Manage—Coach!* course. We offer this course both publicly and privately for organizations, so you can have us come in and take a bunch of your leaders through the course or send them to attend one of our trainings that are open to the public. If you are going to spend money improving your culture, this is the best place to start after having everyone read the book.

At the outset, we talked about the excuses people hold on to that prevent them from creating Dynamic Cultures. Chief among these excuses are: "It is impossible to create a Dynamic Culture in our type of business" and "We can't afford to build a Dynamic Culture." I hope I have demolished and disavowed both of those myths. You can create a Dynamic Culture, and you can afford it. You actually can't afford *not* to create a Dynamic Culture.

Most of what I've taught you, as promised, can be implemented at no cost simply by reorganizing the way you are already doing things. By doing those things you will create new efficiency, bandwidth, and capacity that can be further deployed to improve your culture.

I would also encourage you to start investing financially in your culture, because it sends a clear message to people that it is an organizational and leadership priority.

Tell me the books you are going to read this year and I will tell you how your life will change. Tell me the book that everyone in your organization is going to read this year and I will tell you how your organization will change. Why? We become the books we read. Show me your personal checkbook, your credit card statements, and your personal and professional schedule, and I will tell you what matters most to you. Why? We allocate our time and our money to the things that matter most to us.

If you announce to your organization that creating a Dynamic Culture is an organizational priority but don't spend a penny on it, how do you expect them to believe it? It doesn't need to be a lot of money. Start small and build progressively toward a goal. But have a goal. Decide that within three years you are going to spend 1 percent of revenue or 3 percent of payroll, or whatever number makes sense for your business.

What does "start small" mean? Buy some books and pass them around. Send some of your mangers to the *Don't Just Manage— Coach!* training. There is not a single business or organization on the planet that cannot do these two things, so start there and let's see where it leads you.

Remember the promise I laid out for you in the beginning of this book: *By the end of this book, I hope to have convinced you that culture should be a major priority for you and your organization . . . It is my intention to demonstrate exactly how to go about building a Dynamic Culture that surprises and delights your employees and customers. . . .*

The promise of the book was also set forth to a lesser extent in the subtitle: *A Practical Guide to Building a Dynamic Culture So People Love Coming to Work and Accomplishing Great Things Together!*

Has the book lived up to these promises? Only you can decide. All I know is that to write knowing that so many people in so many places will read your words and take them seriously is both an honor and a tremendous responsibility. It is not one I take lightly, and I hope I have lived up to that responsibility.

Great books are the milestones of people's lives. They remind us of who we are and where we have come from. They point out where we are in our journey right now, and they open our hearts, minds, and souls to new possibilities. Those possibilities are the future—your future.

I pray I have written you a great book here, given you a milestone to look back on fondly from the places you are going in your life and career. But at the very least, I hope I have helped you to see yourself and your business in a new way that will inspire you and the people you toil alongside each day. Thank you for reading. It has been an incredible privilege to write for you.

In closing, I will simply say, give people a healthy environment to work in and they will celebrate you and your organization in ways you have not even begun to imagine. Most organizations only scratch the surface of what they are truly capable of, because they don't give smart, talented, and capable people a healthy environment to work in. Give them a healthy culture and you will be amazed at what together they accomplish.

Are you a little nervous? Good. Are you a little afraid? That's good too. Our nerves and our fear are there to remind us that we are stepping into uncharted territory. Are there monsters and villains in that territory? Maybe, but probably not. The monsters and villains that stop us from living life to the fullest are usually in our minds.

Many leaders are afraid to make cultural changes and scared to hold people accountable. But everyone knows when a culture is sick, and everyone knows when a culture is healthy and dynamic. Most of the time what we fear is just an illusion.

There is a fabulous scene at the end of *The Wizard of Oz*. Dorothy throws water on Scarecrow because he is on fire and she inadvertently splashes water on the Wicked Witch. It turns out that water is the witch's Achilles' heel, and she begins to scream, "I'm melting!" as she disappears in vapors.

As Dorothy and her friends, Lion, Tin Man, and Scarecrow, realize what has happened, their joy quickly turns to fear as they realize that the Wicked Witch's wild flying monkeys have set their stare upon Dorothy. They are naturally afraid that the flying monkeys will turn on Dorothy, attack her, beat her with their lances, or perhaps kill them all.

But the flying monkeys don't. In fact, they do exactly the opposite of what Dorothy, Lion, Tin Man, and Scarecrow expect them to do. "Hail Dorothy!" they all begin to proclaim. They celebrate Dorothy for liberating them from their dictatorial tyrant and the sick culture she created.

I wonder how long the people in your organization have been waiting for someone to come along and say, "We are going to make culture a priority."

The music of a Dynamic Culture is made up of six notes:

1. Make Culture a Priority
2. Mission Is King
3. Overcommunicate the Plan
4. Hire with Rigorous Discipline
5. Let People Know What You Expect
6. Grow Your People by Creating a Coaching Culture

You can do this, and you can start in some small way today. You don't need anyone's permission to improve your culture. I will leave you with a quote from Goethe that I have turned to many times, for many reasons; I hope it inspires you to take action: "Be bold and mighty forces will come to your aid."

Everybody wants a Dynamic Culture, where people love coming to work and accomplishing great things together. Culture is the ultimate competitive advantage.

DO SOMETHING AMAZING!

a matthew kelly company

FLOYD

we grow people.

DON'T JUST MANAGE . . . COACH!

THE CULTURE SOLUTION TRAINING EXPERIENCE

PARTICIPANTS WILL DISCOVER . . .

- Why culture is the ultimate competitive advantage

- The difference between a manager and a Coaching-Leader

- How to become a Coaching-Leader

- How to coach and lead difficult personalities

& more than 21 ways to practically implement the ideas covered in *The Culture Solution* everyday at work!

FLOYD offers this training both as a private training just for your organization, and as a public training open to anyone interested in learning how to become a Coaching-Leader.

1.866.499.2049 | FloydConsulting.com | info@FloydConsulting.com

TRAINING · COACHING · SPEAKING · CONSULTING

are you ready to build a
dynamic culture?

We would love to visit your organization to prepare a culture assessment.

Call us today to
schedule a visit:

Phone:
1.866.499.2049

Email:
info@FloydConsulting.com

TRAINING · COACHING · SPEAKING · CONSULTING

become a
culture
advocate

Sign up today to receive FLOYD'S weekly tips on how you can be the difference that makes the difference in your culture.

www.cultureadvocate.info

THE **MUSIC** OF DYNAMIC CULTURES

is made up of *six notes.*

Learn to play these six notes really well and your culture will become something to

MARVEL AT.

PRINCIPLE 1

Make Culture a PRIORITY

if you activate the other five principles, the first one will *thrive.*

The most effective way to serve everyone's best interests is to make mission king. *Nothing* trumps mission.

MISSION IS KING

PRINCIPLE 2

PRINCIPLE 3

OVERCOMMUNICATE *the Plan.*

When it comes to overcommunication, you will have the *greatest success* if each time you share a message with an individual, your team, or the entire organization, you connect whatever you are trying to say to your organization's common,